# Office Work Measurement

**Harold W. Nance**

*President, Serge A. Birn Company, Division of SABCO, Inc., Louisville, Kentucky*

## Revised Edition

**Robert E. Krieger Publishing Company, Inc.**
**Malabar, Florida**
**1983**

Original Edition 1971
Revised Edition 1983

Printed and Published by
**ROBERT E. KRIEGER PUBLISHING COMPANY, INC.**
**KRIEGER DRIVE**
**MALABAR, FL 32950**

Printed in the United States of America

**Library of Congress Cataloging in Publication Data**

Nance, Harold W.
    Office work measurement.

    Includes index.
     1. Office management. 2. Work measurement.
I. Nolan, Robert E. II. Title.
HF5547.N15    1983    658.3'044    82-20887
ISBN 0-89874-314-1

# Contents

# Foreword

THIS TEXT WILL INTRODUCE the reader to the basic principles that should be considered in an office work measurement program. Even though a particular approach for measuring office work is discussed, it should be remembered that the principles expounded are compatible with all sound approaches for measuring office activities.

In each topic discussed relating to office operations and conditions, the reader should consider the points raised in light of the needs or conditions existing in his or her office. If an illustration or discussion touches close to a condition that needs improving—use it as a starting point to tailor a solution. Hopefully, the discussions will serve to trigger the reader's thoughts to additional solutions.

It should be emphasized that this text has not been written to teach the reader a technique for measuring office work.

Instead, it condenses the experience of many years of working with work measurement programs into explanations of the proper approach and points to be considered in an office work measurement program to improve productivity. Hopefully, it will aid the reader in his or her efforts to measure office work.

Always remember that the most important factor in the equation for improving productivity is people. Without the full support and cooperation of all personnel—from top management down—the efforts to improve productivity in the office will never achieve full success. Therefore, efforts to improve must always emphasize the importance of good communications and human relations between all personnel involved in an office improvement program.

## chapter one

# The Present Situation in the Office

"THE OFFICE CLERICAL FORCE is the poorest "buy" of all corporate expenditures." The exact wording of this statement may have varied slightly depending upon who was making it. Even though it has been made many times, the fact remains that improvements made in the last decade have merely scratched the surface of the potential that still exists.

This leads us to the logical question of "Why haven't these potential savings been realized by the efforts of management?" There is little doubt that one major reason has been management's reluctance to take positive action. Even so, a great deal of the blame can be placed on the confusion created by two opposing and yet compatible disciplines: those of the behavioral scientists and the industrial engineers.

The behavioral scientists preach that the solution to improving productivity in the office area is through creating jobs that motivate employees. The industrial engineers preach that the way to increase productivity is through work measurement and controls. The behavioral scientists pooh-poohed work measurement and controls stating that "Taylorism" is on its way out. On the other hand, the industrial engineers pooh-poohed the importance of creating jobs that motivate and instead went to the extreme of simplifying jobs to the point of boredom.

As a basic result of all this, management has been confused by the direct rhetoric of the two disciplines. Even though they may have started a program meaning to fully support it, this support began to wane when they read opposing statements by the disciplines. The net result is that only a few programs have stayed on course and realized lasting productivity gains.

The true situation existing in the office calls for the marrying of the behavioral science and industrial engineering disciplines. Today's clerical work force is far more sophisticated and better educated than that of several decades ago. This requires much more attention than has been given to programs to reduce office costs in the past.

Most of today's office personnel desire to have a job that will utilize their capabilities and offer them a challenge. As part of this challenge, office employees want to know how they are progressing toward various goals. It is obvious that the creation of jobs that utilize the employees' capabilities and offer a challenge best fits into the work performed by the behavioral scientist. On the other hand, the establishment of a system for reporting to employees how they are doing against established goals is best handled by an industrial engineer. This can be debated by both disciplines; nevertheless, it is this author's opinion that together they would greatly improve the potential productivity gain possible in the office area.

Since this author does not profess to be a behavioral scientist and indeed, is an industrial engineer, this book will be devoted to explaining the work measurement portion of the overall equation to a successful office productivity improvement program.

Unfortunately, many firms have no idea of what work measurement is all about and what it accomplishes. Work measurement, put simply, is the determination of how much time is required to perform a job. Knowing how much time is required, you can then in turn determine from the quantity of work existing for a job how many people or hours will be required to handle the job. Supervisors have long used some form of measurement to determine the staffing needed for their respective departments. This measurement, for the most part, has been based on experience and what past history has indicated, and in most cases, to be on the safe side, supervisors have overstaffed their departments.

On the one hand, productivity has been increased in offices by the efforts of behavioral scientists to create jobs that motivate. For the most part, this increase in productivity has been based on a comparison of what was done by the employees involved prior to redesigning jobs and what was done afterwards. It was not based on what was actually required to do the work prior to and after the redesigning of jobs. On the other hand, the industrial engineer measured office jobs scientifically and reported gains in productivity based on what was actually done before and what should be done. Neither really realized the full potential because neither had completed the full job of truly designing a sound productivity improvement program. Even though jobs have been created that motivate employees, management needs an index to answer the following questions:

1. How effectively are the office employees performing?
2. Is productivity improving?
3. Do we have any trouble spots; if so, where are they?
4. What is the potential capacity of our present office force?

5. What accomplishments have each of my office areas made in relation to economies or efficiency improvements?

These questions have puzzled many executives, and many of them still lack answers.

A good work measurement system will supply the answers needed to these and many other questions, such as:

1. Just what is a fair day's work?
2. How should an uneven work flow be scheduled?
3. Is the organization of our office the best considering the characteristics of the work?
4. Can savings be realized by reducing work requirements?
5. Are employees spending a sufficient amount of time on the skills for which they are being paid?
6. How much does it cost to provide prompt service to customers, and is it worth continuing such a policy?
7. Why has a new method or procedure not produced its hoped-for savings?
8. How long does it take before new employees earn their way?
9. What portion of office expense should be borne by various company products and lines?
10. What should the office performance level be?
11. Are all positions adequately compensated in relation to the duties required on each job?

Actually, work measurement alone will not solve all of the above, but it provides a sound basis for solving most of them.

The situation today is that most offices take the present work paces and conditions for granted, and little or no action has been taken either to improve the working conditions of the employees or to better control what the employee does. Others, however, depend upon improvements to come through systems and procedures or through an electronic data processing system. Both systems and procedures and electronic data processing (EDP) have a place of importance in the overall office productivity equation. However, neither is the sole solution to the problem.

As both fit into the equation, it would be well to discuss how each fits in.

## Where Does Systems and Procedures Analysis Fit In?

The need for improving systems and procedures is not reduced by work measurement. These two endeavors are, in fact, complementary, and the effectiveness of each is enhanced when they are performed simultaneously. The engineering technique used in work measurement is a detailed and systematic analysis of every aspect of an operation—through direct and close observation.

It is impossible to get the "feel" of a procedure in any other way. Through observation, the essence of a system becomes clear, and each operation comes into proper perspective. Desirable changes are thus readily revealed.

Work measurement and systems simplification are different, but inseparable, phases of the same activity. Both in turn provide the basis for making sound decisions on eliminating unnecessary fragmented work.

## The Place of EDP

Electronic data processing (EDP) is being considered almost universally as part of the overall approach to increasing information-handling effectiveness. Some managers have felt that, if needed at all, work simplification and work measurement should come *after* the installation of an EDP system. Is this true? No.

First, the primary basis upon which most computers can be justified is in reduced clerical costs. If we compare postcomputer costs with 50 percent effective precomputer costs, we will always make some erroneous conclusions about computers. Which system to install? Which functions to mechanize?

Second, given the correct computer, it is a mistake to think that all susceptible procedures should be transformed en masse and "as is" to a state of mechanization. This is somewhat like errecting a new plant to build last year's product.

Procedures need trimming and pruning *before* going "on stream" in order to avoid loading the computer with useless information. The "usefulness of every procedure should be challenged before it is electronically perpetuated."

Finally, a computer requires discipline, just as the successful pursuit of any worthwhile program requires discipline. Computers generally are not characterized as flexible. Objectives, plans, and procedures must be put in order for computers to be effective, and standards of quality and performance must be met. A computer cannot exert a last-minute flurry to catch up on work that is late. It relies on regularity, reliability, and adherence to predetermined plans. In short, the computer requires a disciplined administrative group.

A work measurement program also requires discipline and is excellent training for an organization going into a computer program. It is a means of getting the organization "into shape." This conditioning is important to a computer program because a breakdown of procedure discipline results in chaos and sometimes a complete demise of the system. In a work measurement program, however, a temporary breakdown merely causes a delay of benefits.

## Does This Office Situation Sound Familiar?

Sensing that office output isn't what it should be, or by chance happening to see Susie Brown coming in at 9:30 one morning, you decide to do some further checking. After a little "research" you find that Susie is 30 to 40 minutes late reporting to work at least two days each week. You also find that she has a tendency to be 10 to 20 minutes late returning from lunch every day.

This gives you quite a bit of information about Susie, but does it give you the whole story? Do you know what Susie is doing and how well she is doing it during the hours she is at her desk? No. You might be able to say she keeps busy while she is at her desk, but then the question arises, busy at what?

Analyzing this one step further, you may find that Susie has only 4 to 5 hours of real work to do every day. If she knows she has only that much work, this may contribute to the fact that she makes no real effort to be prompt in reporting to work every morning and to get back from lunch on time. After all, human beings have a tendency to become very bored when they have nothing to do. Even though we may follow Parkinson's law and "expand our work to fit the time available," this can become very boring.

## Who Is To Blame?

Managers too often expend effort in the improvement of equipment, forms, and the like and overlook the main resource—*people*. They fail to fully utilize the people available in the office.

Office employees cannot be blamed for not giving a full day's work if they are not told what is expected of them. Neither are the supervisors to blame. Regardless of what excuses we make, it all boils down to the fact that all employees would like to know what is expected of them. Management is at fault, failing to provide supervisors with the proper tools to control production and failing to let people know what is expected of them. And by "what is expected" we mean what is expected in the way of work from each person employed in the office.

The comments made thus far concerning this office situation relate to those of an industrial engineer looking at the job purely from a work measurement point of view. The true situation may have another factor that is causing the difficulty in the office. Perhaps the work being performed is boring, fragmented and therefore offers very little challenge to the employee performing it. In other words, the job itself should be redesigned to motivate the employee. This is where the behavioral scientist comes into play and would play an important part in the overall program. Since our book will deal only with the work measurement aspect, we will state here that looking at the job from the behavioral scientist's point of view would be well worthwhile, as you would accomplish even greater savings by making the job more desirable as well as measuring it.

## Average Performance Before and After Measurement

Surveys of offices have definitely indicated that most employees feel they could do more work than they are presently doing. This validates the results of work measurement, which have indicated the same results that employees state. Our experience has indicated that most offices without a work measurement or motivation program perform at best around 55 percent of the full potential available. A survey performed by our firm among 10 companies seems to verify this statement. In fact, the 55 percent based on these 10 is some 2 percent high. The results can be seen on Figure 1-1, Summary of Results of Office Improvement Program.

In referring to Figure 1-1, you will note that the weighted average performance prior to the installation of work measurement with controls was 53 percent, and 81 percent after the installation of work measurement and controls. As you must agree, this is a sizable increase.

To really get a feel for the savings made, suppose the cost per hour for each employee was $5. This means that prior to

| A | B | C | D | E | F |
|---|---|---|---|---|---|
| | TOTAL CONTROLLABLE EMPLOYEES | PERFORMANCE %'s | | | |
| COMPANY | | PRIOR TO CONTROLS | | AFTER CONTROLS | |
| | | GROUP | WEIGHTED B x C | GROUP | WEIGHTED B x E |
| 1 | 55 | 62 | 34.10 | 81 | 44.55 |
| 2 | 450 | 60 | 270.00 | 83 | 373.50 |
| 3 | 605 | 41 | 248.05 | 77 | 465.85 |
| 4 | 700 | 53 | 371.00 | 90 | 630.00 |
| 5 | 335 | 59 | 197.65 | 86 | 288.10 |
| 6 | 31 | 50 | 15.50 | 72 | 22.32 |
| 7 | 197 | 50 | 98.50 | 82 | 161.54 |
| 8 | 300 | 50 | 150.00 | 72 | 216.00 |
| 9 | 350 | 60 | 210.00 | 93 | 325.50 |
| 10 | 1000 | 55 | 550.00 | 75 | 750.00 |
| Total | 4023 | | 2144.80 | | 3277.36 |
| Average | 402 | | 53.3 | | 81.5 |

Figure 1-1. Summary of Results of Office Improvement Program.

the installation of work measurement and controls the productive output actually cost $9.43 per hour ($5/hr. ÷ 53% performance). After the installation of work measurement and controls, the cost of productive work was $6.17 per hour ($5/h. ÷ 81%). This obviously would result in a savings per hour of $3.26 ($9.43 − $6.17). A good savings, I am sure you will agree.

In referring to Figure 1-1, you will note that the performance after controls ranges from 72 percent to 93 percent. Also, you will note that the number of employees in the office area ranges from 31 to 1,000. This means that work measurement and controls would benefit both the small and large office areas. Again, however, it should be pointed out that had behavioral science techniques been combined with work measurement, the "after controls," performance level would have been some 8 percent to 10 percent higher.

## Summary of Present Conditions

To summarize, the condition in today's offices needs both the behavioral science approach and that of the industrial engineer. The behavioral scientist's approach is needed to create jobs that motivate, and the industrial engineer is needed to determine how many people are required to adequately staff these jobs and to provide meaningful feedback to the employees.

With the increasing need for improving productivity in our nation, both work measurement and motivation have a very important place in the office if offices are to remain competitive and provide meaningful employment in the future.

chapter two

# Can Scientific Management Be Applied?

WITH THE CONDITIONS that exist in the office, the big question is "Can scientific management be applied?" The obvious answer is yes; however, it must be applied with a far different approach than has been taken in the past.

Before discussing this different approach to applying scientific management, we should define the term. Frederick W. Taylor, the father of scientific management, defines "scientific management" as "management based on measurement plus control." This definition makes good sense in anything we do. However, the proliferation of events attributed to scientific management has resulted in the need for a different approach to applying scientific management.

In everything you and I do, we have some form of measurement and some kind of controls involved. A prime example is going from home to work. Without realizing it, each of us has determined how long on the average it takes to cover the distance and in turn has allotted that time to get to work. Our control is that we know when we must leave home, and more often than not we watch that time very carefully. We also watch the time in relation to arrival at work and become very annoyed when something interferes to prevent either being met.

The time to go from our home to work is in essence a standard we have set for ourselves. We set the standard by our experience in driving, riding buses or trains, etc. Even though we did not realize it, when we decided that it will take us 1 hour to go from home to work, we have actually established a standard for going to work. Our control is making sure we meet the standard that has been set.

In establishing our 1 hour standard, we included time to purchase the daily newspaper and leisurely read it while waiting for our transportation and riding to work. In our job, knowing what is going on locally as well as internationally is important. By reading the newspaper each morning, we are aware of what is going on by the time we reach our office. In analyzing our daily routine, we find that by not purchasing the newspaper each morning and leisurely reading it while waiting for our transportation to arrive we can sleep 15 minutes longer, as it will take us only 45 minutes to get to work. So, we decided to eliminate the newspaper and sleep the extra 15 minutes.

After about a week of our new routine, we become upset and start to lose interest in our work because our associates are discussing things we are not aware of. It turns out that they are discussing items that have appeared in the paper that affect the operation of the business. Due to our elimination of reading the newspaper each morning to get 15 more minutes sleep, we have lost contact with what is going on.

Believe it or not, this example, though somewhat exaggerated, is exactly what many of us practitioners of scientific management have done to jobs in the office area. In order to save time, we have too often eliminated the activities of the job which provide the employee with a feeling of importance and being needed as part of the team. These changes were often made to speed up the flow of paper without regard to what effect they had on the overall attitude of the employee performing the work.

For years office employees accepted this approach and there was very little apparent dissatisfaction. However, as our employees became better educated overall, we found that our productivity began to suffer. Therefore, in order to apply scientific management properly, we must measure and control jobs that provide meaningful and challenging work to the employee. With this in mind, we will now discuss how scientific management can be applied.

Once jobs have been designed so they will properly utilize the ability of our employees, scientific management—measurement and controls—definitely has its place. Its place is to provide a meaningful goal for the employees to attain and feedback (reporting) to indicate how they are progressing toward that goal. The control would be periodic checks of true progress and discussions with employees.

To establish meaningful goals will require developing of standards based on some form of work measurement. We will now discuss standards and work measurement.

## Standards

A standard in work measurement terms is the time required to perform a fixed amount of work by a prescribed method at a normal work pace. The standard as such normally contains an allowance to provide for coffee breaks, getting a drink of water, going to the rest room, short interruptions, etc. This allowance is normally referred to as a PF&D allowance or

PR&D allowance—meaning personal, fatigue, and unavoidable delay or personal, rest, and unavoidable delay.

We will discuss normal, methods and allowances in further detail.

**Normal**    Normal is defined as a work pace that can be maintained all day without undue fatigue. The clincher in this definition is "undue fatigue." The author, as do many others, has difficulty in defining the word fatigue as it relates to work measurement. Therefore, for our purposes we will define normal as a pace that can be maintained all day without becoming tired.

Normal in work measurement is also referred to as the 100 percent performance level. Therefore, if the normal time for performing a particular office job is 1 hour and an employee doing the job takes 1 hour to perform it, then the employee's performance is 100 percent ($1 \div 1$) or normal. On the other hand, if the employee took 1¼ hours to perform a job with a normal time of 1 hour, then the employee would be performing at below normal (100 percent ) or at 80 percent ($1 \div 1¼$). Figure 2-1 is the comparison of normal with the various performances you can expect in the office.

Even though 100 percent is considered normal in an office where standards are used for improving goals of employees, you will note that 70 percent is the acceptable minimum performance limit on Figure 2-1. Above 100 percent on Figure 2-1 you will see reference to an incentive pace. This is due to the fact that performances of over 100 percent are normally connected with some form of extra compenstation to the employees.

**Method**    Method is defined as the proper way of performing a job so as to eliminate unnecessary motions. It is this area of scientific management that has often been oversimplified by the industrial engineer. In our efforts to eliminate unneces-

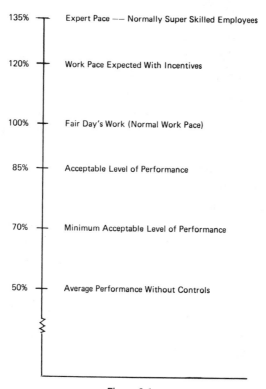

Figure 2-1

sary motions, we often split jobs into smaller components so it would be easy to teach employees how to perform them by the proper method.

Our method improvements very often resulted in what the behavioral scientists call fragmented jobs. That is, the jobs lost meaning and relationship for the persons performing them. Therefore, we should redefine "method" as developing a job made up of meaningful components that best utilize the capabilities of the employees assigned.

With this as our goal in developing methods, we should still look at unnecessary motions as well as all other aspects of the job but not to the point where the job becomes meaningless.

**Allowances**    Allowances in work measurement were created
to provide for the normal time lost by an employee during a
workday. Each person at some time during the workday will
need time for personal needs (rest room, drink of water, etc.).
He/she will also need time for the "coveted" coffee breaks and
for minor interruptions that occur from time to time which
are no more than 4 or 5 minutes in duration. All of these
combined were originally called PF&D allowance—meaning
personal, fatigue, and delay allowance. The author, however,
prefers to call it a PR&D allowance—meaning personal, rest,
and delay allowance.

The allowance is added to the normal time for performing
a job to arrive at what is known as the standard. The allowance is usually expressed as a percent of the available working
time in a day. For example, if you determine in your firm that
the following time will be lost in an 8 hour day:

| Item | Time Lost in Hours |
| --- | --- |
| Personal | .30 |
| Coffee Breaks | .50 |
| Minor Delays | .45 |
| Total Lost: | 1.25 hours |

then your allowance would be 1.25 hours ÷ (8 hrs − 1.25 hrs.)
or 18.5 percent.

This means your employees have only 6.75 hours
(8 − 1.25) available to perform their jobs. If the normal time
for a job was 1 hour, then each employee could perform only
6.75 jobs in an 8 hour day. On the other hand, we could add
the 18.5 percent allowance to the 1 hour and obtain a standard of 1.185 hours per job. This would result in only 6.75
jobs in an 8 hour day (8 ÷ 1.185). Allowance, as such, then
makes up for time that will normally be lost by the employee
in a normal workday. Other forms of allowance also exist, but
for now we will deal only with this basic allowance.

## Techniques for Measuring Clerical Work

To measure clerical work, a unit of time is developed for producing a defined unit of output. In other words, clerical work measurement is concerned with identifying the units of output produced and determining the amount of time needed to produce each unit of output. The results of determining this, as we will see later, provide you with a means of developing systems for reporting the actual output and comparing actual effort against absolute values for the work performed.

There are many techniques used in setting standards. The basic types are historical data, work sampling, time study, and predetermined time systems. These basic types have several variations which are discussed below, and it is not uncommon to combine two or more basic approaches or their variations in one program.

**Historical Data**   Historical data studies involve accumulating information about time and output from records connected with the operation of a clerical unit. An average time per unit of work is calculated, and it may be either used as it is derived or adjusted to form tighter or looser standards by using mathematical adjustment formulas. These formulas represent an attempt to rate the pace or speed at which an employee is working against what is considered "average." Adjustments may also take the form of increasing the standards by choosing to consider only the faster times when computing the average.

It is the easiest and most frequently used technique. For example, suppose the billing department consists of three people each working 8 hours per day. We can then state that billing requires 24 hours per day. If billing turns out an average of 100 invoices per day, we can calculate that each invoice requires 0.24 hour, or 14.4 minutes each. This would be a standard based on past history.

Many times historical data studies are made only to provide an analysis of a clerical unit's time. When procedures change very little, it is possible to use this "one-shot" study with some accuracy and little upkeep. When procedures or conditions change, it may be necessary to repeat the study at intervals in order to maintain the validity of the study.

This repetition may occur at regular intervals, at irregular intervals, at the request of the supervisor, or when it is known that methods or conditions have changed.

While this is the simplest form of measurement, it also tends to be the least accurate because it is based on the current staff and current conditions and does not require a particularly detailed definition of methods. In the above example with the billing of invoices, we do not know under what conditions the 100 invoices were originally prepared; we do not know if the method of invoicing is up to date and efficient; and we do not know how the employees in this department performed when they processed the 100 invoices.

This is better than having no standard at all. It does provide a measurement and control over what is going on in your office, although it may not be very accurate or precise. The biggest fallacy is that it shows you what you *have* done and not what you *should* have done.

Historical clerical measurement could be your first step to control clerical costs. It should not be your last.

**Work Sampling**    Work sampling is based on observation of employees at work according to statistically valid observation tables. There are two kinds of work sampling: ratio delay and sampling.

Ratio delay involves observing the employees to determine if they are working or not working. These data can then be used to add or subtract load from a clerical unit.

Other forms of sampling involve listing some basic tasks that are performed in the clerical unit and then making random observations to determine the frequency with which they occur. This sampling is converted into percentages of time and finally minutes or hours spent on the various tasks. The volume of output for each task can be divided into the sample time to construct a standard. Because work sampling can be used to determine the amount of idle time in an area, it tends to be somewhat more accurate in rating the pace of an employee than historical data.

The basic methods of work sampling can be determined from most office administrative manuals or texts on work measurement. Work sampling, however, is limited to rather gross observation. It is normally used to evaluate a relatively small number of tasks, and then it does not usually take into account either methods or conditions.

There are many programs involving a combination of historical data and work sampling. Historical data are usually acceptable to the clerical employees and supervisors because they represent their actual peformance and present conditions, so they can become a basic form of work measurement. When work sampling is used to determine the *pace* of a clerical unit, the data collected from a historical study can be adjusted by the percentage of idle time from the work sampling study. In this way two simple approaches are combined into an acceptable form of work measurement that allows for employee work pace.

**Time Study**   Time study, or the observation and careful timing of observed work, is probably the oldest technique of work measurement. It involves defining a job in terms of its elements and making careful observations (usually using a stopwatch) to set the time for the element. The time study analyst—usually someone who has professional training and experience in this aspect of measurement—rates the pace of the person performing the operation. A number of observations consistent with the length of the job and its complexity are made to assure statistical accuracy.

Because this method has been used in the factory for many

years, it has wide acceptance there, and it is considered very accurate. Unfortunately, this strength is also its weakness: time study, and the use of a stopwatch, has generally proved psychologically unacceptable to office personnel.

The three main disadvantages of time study are inconsistent standards, high cost, and omission of methods analysis. Since they involve the subjective element of performance rating (assessing the work pace of an operator), time study standards can be inconsistent. Time study requires many observations to get accurate times for establishing clerical standards. And the time study analyst is usually more concerned with what the employee *is* doing than what the employee *should* be doing.

**Motion Pictures**    Another approach to measurement involves use of a motion picture camera and micromotion analysis. This is very costly and time-consuming, but it does furnish a good description of the method being used and a great deal of detail concerning the operation.

Taking movies in the office may be very objectionable and may cause morale problems. If you want to use this technique, be sure to prepare the employees at least a day or so ahead of time. We can't recommend using the camera for clerical work measurement. It's too costly unless you apply the data derived to many offices throughout your company.

Rather than using motion pictures for developing standards, you may want to consider them for training purposes. They are also an ideal way of transferring information from one office to another.

**Predetermined Times**    So-called "canned" data, or predetermined times, are a catalog of clerical work elements that can be applied to approximately 95 percent of office work. In this approach you obtain all your information for measuring clerical work through *discussions* with office supervision and employees. During these discussions you learn what people do, how they do it, and what is done with the work once they have completed it. You have a detailed description of the methods used and the work produced.

From predetermined times not only can you develop a standard for the way a job is presently being done, but you can analyze it and, many times, improve the methods used. This type of clerical measurement serves two purposes. It gives you a *time* for performing an operation and the basis for improving the *method*.

Of all the tools available, we personally feel that a standard data system based on predetermined time is best. With it you can record all details concerning a job, so that you can later analyze it for methods improvements. You also have, as a by-product, the updating of any job descriptions involved in your job evaluation for wage and salary administration.

## Summary

When you choose the tool or technique to be used by your firm to develop clerical standards, be sure it is easy to explain to your management and *can be sold to them.*

Remember, to control office costs, you must have standards. And you must be able to economically update these standards when changes occur.

## chapter three

# Myths That Must Be Overcome

THE TREND TOWARD THE office area becoming a bigger and bigger part of our overall cost of doing business makes it imperative to improve the productivity level. Economists predict that this will be the frontier of the future—improving productivity gains to provide our national growth.

Even so, many managers are reluctant to take positive action to improve. After all, office activities have traditionally been considered a necessary cost of operating a business, and few have questioned the true productivity level of this important part of the business picture. However, in the coming years management must take action to remain competitive in both the domestic and international markets.

The domestic and international markets are no longer separate. Whether or not we want to admit it, everything we do today is competitive domestically with either foreign or foreign-controlled firms. Thus, management and supervision must face the fact that improving productivity in the office is a must for survival.

A sound approach to improvement is obviously introducing work measurement to determine and control work loads. Even when a good program of designing jobs that motivate has been installed, you need to know how long each job takes in order to properly provide meaningful goals for the employees. Managers and supervisors will often give as excuses for not introducing measurement one of the following myths.

## The Creativity Myth

The managers who say, "That job requires creative ability and therefore cannot be measured," oftentimes base their statement on conditions that surrounded a particular job or jobs at some phase in the company's development. For example, they may have at one time held the job in question. At that time all the procedures surrounding this job may well have had to be "created." However, once these procedures were created, the job no longer required creative ability as we know it.

Now, let's analyze the word "creative," as many people in both management and areas of business often misuse this word. The word "creative" is defined in the dictionary as "having the power or quality of creating." Another meaning of this word that would fit the situation more appropriately is "having the ability to produce something new or different and not something that is an imitation or a variation of something that is already being done."

Very few of our office employees really perform work of a creative nature. Even those who do can be measured and are measured by some method. For example, a growing area in the office has involved systems analysts or computer programmers who develop the means by which a firm utilizes the computer. Even though it is not true work measurement, some form of measurement has been used to determine how many personnel are needed to handle this function. We can naturally argue whether the measurement was right or wrong, but nevertheless some method of measurement was used.

In essence, creativity is not a valid excuse for not developing some form of work measurement to establish meaningful goals. Also, it is doubtful as to how much creativity actually exists in the majority of the work performed in the office.

## The Judgment Myth

Another objection from supervisors concerns a job they say calls for "judgment." And, they say, since you cannot measure thinking time or mental processes, you cannot measure such a job.

Getting back to the dictionary again, "judgment" is defined as "a formal utterance or pronouncement of an authoritative opinion after judging," and "to judge" is "to have knowledge sufficient to decide on the merits of a question." Actually, the word "judgment" is misused by many people to define decisions of the "yes" and "no" category. People confuse a simple decision with a judgment.

In all jobs people are called on to make decisions; however, these decisions are not what we would call "judgment." For example, take the case of the executive who dictates a memo on a specific subject and forgets to tell the typist who should get copies. When the typist gets this memo, she will probably make the decision. But is this really a "judgment"? Her decision as to who gets copies is based on past experience. Many people confuse judgment with experience.

People who refer to "creativity" and "judgment" usually mean simply that the job requires some form of thinking. If procedures are properly established, very little if any deep thinking should be required to do the jobs performed by clerical office employees. With proper training, all employees should know how to handle each phase of their job. They should not have to stop to figure out the next thing to do.

The type of deep thinking we are talking about in reference to creativity and judgment is where a person might stare off into space, scratch his head, and start all the wheels rolling in his mind to figure out what to do. While we will find a large number of people who appear to be doing this, it is more the reason why the job *should* be measured than not!

Here is the position to take on the question of "judgment." First, put the type of decision making one has to do in its proper perspective. Is it the kind of decision making one has to do when buying a new suit? That is more like admiring, isn't it? We don't find clerical employees having to strain out decisions like that.

Recognize that all tasks require some degree of mental control and "think" time. In situations that call for "having knowledge sufficient to decide on the merits of a question," recognize that thought processes occur simultaneously with mental and physical actions such as reading and writing. While we are reading or writing, we are also simultaneously evaluating and judging. The accuracy of the judgment does not require a separate time period devoid of all physical effort whereby we must act like Rodin's "Thinker" before arriving at a decision.

If enough time is provided for reading, writing, or listening to information, then the decision becomes of the "yes" and "no" variety and is therefore measureable.

Part of the blame for the exaggerated sophistication of some jobs rests with management because of the fancy titles attached to many of the jobs. Some companies give titles instead of money. And people tend to mistake the importance of a job by the title given. Here are some examples of seemingly descriptive yet actually exaggerated titles:

*Copywriter*: proofreads copy returned from the printer to make sure that it corresponds with the original copy sent by the company's advertising agency.

*Accountant*: checks or prepares statistics for use in a computer program.

*Sales Representative*: handles requests for sales literature.

Or take the difference between an accountant and a bookkeeper. A true accountant is a person who analyzes expense charges and decides in which account they should be put for the company to maintain meaningful books, obtain the best break on taxes, etc. A bookkeeper, on the other hand, is the person who posts these expenses once a decision has been made as to where they are to be posted.

A true copywriter is a person who creates copy and writes it, not the person just described above.

A great deal of the misconception of true creativity and judgment is due to the titles given to various jobs throughout offices.

## The Morale Myth

Another myth is, "If you try to improve my operation you will upset the morale of my employees." Or, "This is the wrong time to conduct a study of our operations because we are automating and two changes would really upset morale."

What these people are really saying is, "I don't want to rock the boat." "Leave well enough alone."

Aren't they really saying that they are afraid of the scientific management movement because they might be required to exhibit some ability to manage? It is very true that people resent change. However, without change, we do not progress.

Employees like to be recognized and to have an opportunity to discuss their work. The majority of them would like to know what is expected of them. Employees who have something useful to do all day are much happier than those who have to expand their work to fit the time available.

Now, let's take a typical office and see just what measurement would do to morale. In most offices, you will find varying degrees of the following:

1. Employees who keep busy from the time they arrive at the office until the time they leave—they even assist others in their work in order to stay busy.
2. Employees who handle everything meticulously and make sure their work is expanded to fit the time available.
3. Employees who work very hard the first part of the day and then spread out their work so that they can take time for coffee, rest room, and social breaks.
4. Employees who have difficulty in doing their job and must always check with the supervisor on every detail.

These examples do not include *all* the employees in offices, but they will serve to illustrate how measurement affects morale.

The first employee is the one who keeps busy all day even if it involves taking work from other people in order to fill out his day. When measured, this employee is normally pinpointed as one of the outstanding workers within a department, and if supervision is on the ball, they will let the employee know that he is outstanding.

The employee feels happier and more pleased with himself. He now knows that *management* knows what he is doing, and he does not feel that his good work is unrecognized. Employees in this category have been very elated over the fact that a system has been installed to let management know what they have been doing. They are also happy to know that management will take some action to give other people a more even work load.

The second employee (who does his work meticulously and

expands his work to fit the time available) nine times out of ten will be relieved to know that he will not have to stretch out his work, but will be given enough work to keep him busy all day. The normal office worker would prefer to have something to do all day rather than spending his time trying to stretch it out merely to look busy.

On numerous occasions, employees explain that they are very happy to know that management finally has a way of determining how much work can be done and is now assigning work that will keep them busy throughout the day. They say that work that keeps them busy all day makes the day much shorter.

The third category finds employees who work very rapidly in the morning and then spread out the remainder of work over the day so that they can take as many coffee, rest room, and social breaks as they would like. You might expect these employees to have a great dislike for measurement, but such is not the case. Many of them would really like to know how much is expected of them and would perform what is expected and take their coffee breaks after this is done.

The last category is the worker who always has difficulty and is always conferring with the supervisor as to what to do. This worker is usually the person who is a misfit in the job. Measurement readily points out employees who lack the skill, dexterity, or ability to perform certain jobs.

A poor attitude toward measurement on the part of the supervisor can have a bad effect on employee morale. The only way to solve this problem is for management to take a firm stand on measurement when they introduce it, not be wishy-washy about whether it will be installed or not. On the other hand, those who install measurement must do a much better job of educating supervision in just what work measurement is all about. They should explain to them how it is done, what the results look like, how they can make use of it, and above all how they can become part of the work measurement program.

In summary, we find morale improves after the installation of a clerical measurement program for several reasons. Employees are *happier* when they (1) get recognition for good performance, (2) have a balanced work load and are therefore not underloaded or overloaded, (3) have bottlenecks eliminated so work flows more smoothly, and (4) know that salary increases and merit ratings are based on objective rather than subjective considerations.

One last statement that should be made in relation to morale is that the manager or supervisor may already have a morale problem. This morale problem could easily be the result of poorly designed and fragmented jobs that result in low production, absenteeism, and turnover. In this case, both redesigning of the jobs and work measurement are needed.

## The Quality Myth

The general feeling of supervisors and managers who have had no experience with work measurement is that the quality of work suffers. Their opinion is that employees speed up in their work pace, causing an undue number of errors. The truth of the matter is that employees do not speed up their operation, because, generally, people cannot speed up more than 10 percent.

Production improves under a measurement program, not as a result of faster motions, but rather as a result of encouraging employees to apply themselves more *continuously* to the job and to avoid time-consuming personal interruptions. Our experience is that a lower percentage of errors occurs when employees are working under a measurement program because they are applying themselves to their work rather than daydreaming as they are doing the job.

The argument is heard that quality will be sacrificed for quantity. This simply is not so. It is just another way of saying, perhaps, that if a supervisor cannot control the number of errors he presently has, what will he do when production increases? As a result, a supervisor will pacify himself with old sayings like "haste makes waste" and "slow but sure"—which does nothing more than dignify gross ineffectiveness. Stated very simply, errors and poor quality of work increase only when a supervisor permits them to increase.

Experience has definitely established that there is *no correlation whatsoever between higher productivity and lower quality.* People who work at a slower pace often make more errors than faster employees. A favorable smooth rhythm pattern for doing the work will produce more work accurately. Errors germinate from poor placement, inadequate training, and poor attitudes. If an individual is asked to work harder and thereby produces more errors, chances are that there was a higher proportion of poor quality at the lower rate of output. Don't try to lower or remove the standard, but examine the methods used and provide the employee with the help and instruction needed.

Quality is more often than not directly connected with the employee's interest in his or her work. Therefore, when a manager or supervisor states as part of the quality myth "that we have difficulty enough with quality without introducing measurement that will call for more work," he or she is saying that their employees are not happy performing the work. This is a definite area where jobs need redesigning.

## The Union Myth

Back to the subject of measurement and morale, it would be well to comment that one of the most common objections to measurement is that it will bring unionization of the office. *We know of no office that can blame measurement as such for their having a union.* While there are offices that have been unionized as a result of the way measurement has been used, you will agree that the measurement itself cannot be blamed when people misuse it.

## The Wrong Time Myth

The first fallacy here is that automation precedes measurement. "We don't want to bother with measurement now; we are automating and will get our savings this way." Then, when they are deeply involved in the automation project, we hear, "We are too busy working the bugs out of the system to even talk about measurement."

Measurement gives you an opportunity to straighten out methods and procedures. There are two popular axioms in EDP: "You cannot automate a mess," and "Garbage in, garbage out."

In a formal program there is a three-step process: analysis, measurement, and control. Analysis of the work for the best method, distribution, flow, and layout allows for organization of the work in the best possible way. Measurement is applied to the better system. And controls enable you to make improvements and maintain them.

At this point, any attempt to cost out a system preparatory to automation will

1. Involve readily available cost figures from existing standards.
2. Provide more accurate and realistic savings (if any) figures, since all the "fat" was taken out after measurement.

## chapter four

# Planning an Office Improvement Program

THE PROPER PLANNING of an office improvement program is an essential step in making it a complete success. Before planning starts, however, all members of the management team must fully support improving your office operations. This support must be genuine and not lip service. As you are well aware, many people state they fully support nearly every idea introduced by their superiors. In reality, many might see only "death and taxes" as being inarguable and inescapable.

Once full support of an office improvement program is assured, then plans must be made:

1. For the basic elements that will be included in your office improvement program, and
2. How these basic elements will be carried out.

We will discuss each of these as basic program elements and program implementation.

## Basic Program Elements

An ideal office improvement program would consist of the following elements:

1. Redesigning of jobs so that the resulting job will motivate employees;
2. Measuring of each job performed; and
3. Establishing of feedback (reporting) and controls for determining the progress of employees or departments.

From these three elements, other elements you may desire can result, such as standard costing of services, bonus or incentive plans, salary reviews, budgeting of manpower, etc.

Redesigning of jobs so that the resulting jobs provide motivation to employees requires providing basic behavioral science assistance to all levels of management. It then involves management working with employees to develop jobs that will provide meaningful and challenging work that will fully utilize the ability of the employees. To accomplish this will require a willingness on the part of management to relinquish some areas of what they may have previously felt were their responsibilities. You can obtain a much better feel for this important element of a sound program by reading texts prepared by experts who have actually been involved in the implementation of motivational programs. Dr. Robert N. Ford has two excellent texts[1] that will give you an insight into this important subject.

Another important element to be considered in planning your program is that of being able to measure each of the jobs performed in your office. This requires a decision on your part as to the kind of measurement system you wish to use. As

[1]*Motivation Through The Work Itself*, by Robert N. Ford, 1969, published by American Management Association, Inc. *Why Jobs Die & What To Do About It—Job Redesign and Future Productivity* by Robert N. Ford, 1979, AMACOM.

we discussed in the previous chapter, several measurement systems are available. More than likely a sound program will require one basic system for measuring the majority of the work performed with occasional use of other techniques to measure special activities. For example, if you used predetermined office data, you will probably need a stopwatch to obtain machine or process times and possibly work sampling to determine frequencies and allowances. To refresh your memory, the chart on Figure 4-1 will review briefly the most prominent measurement approaches.

Once the first two elements of your program are decided on, then you must decide if you wish feedback (reporting) and controls on an employee or a departmental basis. On an employee basis, each employee will report how she or he spent the work week. This results in providing a performance level for each employee.

On a departmental basis, how the time of the department is

Pros and Cons of the Five Clerical Work Measurement Techniques

| TECHNIQUE | PRO | CON | COMMENT |
|---|---|---|---|
| Historical Data | Gives some degree of control. | Imprecise. | A good first step. |
| Work Sampling | Helpful in pinpointing best areas for detailed study. | Involves dangerous assumptions regarding "work." | Fine for determining allowances and frequencies. |
| Time Study | Actually measures work. | Requires subjective rating and use of hated stopwatch. Factory overtones. Usually omits method description. | Useful in spot-checking standards developed by other methods. Essential for process or machine times. |
| Motion Pictures | Provides detailed, easily understood description and record of method. | Costly and time-consuming. "On camera" problems. | Valuable as a teaching aid for new employees. |
| Predetermined Times | Fast, easy to apply. Eliminates feeling of being studied. | Danger of misapplication because of apparent simplicity. | Best applied in streamlined form rather than basic predetermined time data. |

Figure 4-1

WEEKLY PERFORMANCE REPORT

| DEPARTMENT CORPORATE SERVICES | | SECTION DOCUMENT PROCESSING | | | | SUPERVISOR SUE DOWNES | | WEEK ENDING 7-11-99 | |
|---|---|---|---|---|---|---|---|---|---|
| EMPLOYEE | HOURS | | | | | | | % COVERAGE (H)(H÷F+G) | % PERFORMANCE (AXB)(H) |
| | TOTAL (C) | ABSENT/ LOANED (D) | SUPERVISORY (E) | UNMEASURED NO STD. (F) | OTHER (G) | ACTUAL (H) | STANDARD (AXB) | | |
| Grace Eden | 40.0 | | | | 3.1 | 36.9 | 39.4 | 92 | 107 |
| Edna Brown | 40.0 | 8.0 | | | 6.6 | 25.4 | 26.3 | 79 | 104 |
| Joyce Adams | 40.0 | | | 3.5 | 1.5 | 35.0 | 35.0 | 88 | 100 |
| Laura Root | 40.0 | | | | 4.3 | 35.7 | 34.5 | 89 | 97 |
| Kathy Hunt | 40.0 | 12.0 | | | 2.6 | 25.4 | 21.6 | 91 | 85 |
| Ann Frank | 40.0 | | 13.5 | 2.0 | 1.6 | 22.9 | 18.5 | 86 | 81 |
| Eileen Love | 40.0 | | | | 6.4 | 33.6 | 25.5 | 84 | 76 |
| Paula Iris | 40.0 | | | 4.2 | 11.3 | 24.5 | 17.6 | 61 | 72 |
| Lois Quett | 40.0 | | | | | 40.0 | 28.6 | 100 | 72 |
| Karen Pope | 40.0 | 10.0 | | 1.5 | 6.0 | 22.5 | 15.6 | 75 | 69 |
| Jackie Kerin | 40.0 | 2.0 | | | 7.4 | 30.6 | 19.9 | 81 | 65 |
| Sue Downes | 40.0 | | 38.0 | | 2.0 | 0.0 | 0.0 | -- | -- |
| | | | | | | | | | |
| | | | | | | | | | |
| | | | | | | | | | |
| | | | | | | | | | |
| (12)   TOTALS | 480.0 | 32.0 | 51.5 | 11.2 | 52.8 | 332.5 | 282.5 | 84 | 85 |

REMARKS

Figure 4-2

WEEKLY PERFORMANCE SUMMARY REPORT

| DEPARTMENT Corporate Services | | SECTION Document Processing | | | | | CCC | SUPERVISOR Sue Downes | | |
|---|---|---|---|---|---|---|---|---|---|---|
| WEEK ENDING | TOTAL EMPLOYEES ASSIGNED | HOURS | | | | | | | % COVERAGE | % PERFORMANCE |
| | | TOTAL | ABSENT/ LOANED | SUPERVISORY | UNMEASURED NO STANDARD | OTHER | ACTUAL | STANDARD | | |
| 4-18-99 | 16 | 672.0 | 40.0 | 55.0 | 22.3 | 12.4 | 542.3 | 276.3 | 94 | 51 |
| 4-25-99 | 16 | 660.0 | 41.5 | 52.0 | 22.0 | 2.8 | 541.7 | 281.4 | 96 | 52 |
| 5-2-99 | 16 | 652.0 | 42.0 | 55.0 | 23.6 | 5.0 | 526.4 | 280.3 | 95 | 53 |
| 5-9-99 | 15 | 635.0 | 42.0 | 57.5 | 6.8 | 2.0 | 526.7 | 276.9 | 98 | 54 |
| 5-16-99 | 15 | 610.0 | 31.0 | 51.0 | 4.0 | .5 | 523.5 | 284.1 | 99 | 54 |
| 5-23-99 | 15 | 600.0 | 82.5 | 53.0 | 4.3 | 3.4 | 456.8 | 277.5 | 98 | 61 |
| 5-29-99 | 14 | 582.0 | 65.8 | 52.0 | 6.2 | 4.2 | 453.8 | 281.8 | 98 | 62 |
| 6-6-99 | 14 | 560.0 | 60.0 | 53.5 | 6.0 | 2.0 | 438.5 | 280.3 | 98 | 64 |
| 6-13-99 | 13 | 530.0 | 40.0 | 50.0 | 8.1 | 20.4 | 411.5 | 282.6 | 94 | 69 |
| 6-20-99 | 13 | 530.0 | 66.3 | 51.5 | 7.8 | 37.2 | 367.0 | 279.4 | 89 | 76 |
| 6-27-99 | 13 | 530.0 | 44.0 | 50.0 | 9.2 | 27.8 | 389.0 | 281.0 | 91 | 72 |
| 7-4-99 | 12 | 484.0 | 40.0 | 54.0 | 7.6 | 50.0 | 332.4 | 280.0 | 85 | 84 |
| 7-11-99 | 12 | 480.0 | 32.0 | 51.5 | 11.2 | 52.8 | 332.5 | 282.5 | 84 | 85 |

COMMENTS

| ISSUED BY C. Campbell, Mgr., Work Measurement | DATE 7-13-99 | |
|---|---|---|

Figure 4-3

spent and what was produced is reported, and the result is an overall performance of the department. Figures 4-2 and 4-3 are examples of individual employee and departmental reports.

For either individual or departmental feedback (reporting), methods must be established whereby the information reported actually represents what was done. This means we must establish methods by which we can audit production counts and times reported. Without some checks and balances, either individual or departmental feedback (reporting) can often be misleading. We plan on discussing this in more detail in another chapter.

Once we have established what the basic elements of our office improvement program will be, then we must determine how these elements will be carried out in our firm. We will now discuss the alternates available for carrying out an office improvement program.

## How To Carry Out the Basic Program Elements

Several alternates are available for carrying out your office improvement program basic elements. These alternates are:

1. Hire a staff of personnel with previous experience to carry out such a program;
2. Hire some key staff with previous experience in handling such a program and let them develop additional needed personnel from within to carry out your program;
3. Select your office control staff from within and have an outside consultant assist in developing this staff and your program; or
4. Use an outside consultant to carry out your entire program.

Each of these can in turn be modified to create other alternates; however, for our purpose we will limit our comments to these four.

Hiring a staff with previous office control experience can become a very difficult task, as it would almost involve pirating of the staff of one or two firms to fulfill your needs. It can also become costly in the long-range picture, as you will normally need to offer a much higher salary and benefit package to attract the needed staff. By doing this you may upset the pay structure not only for your firm but for all firms in your area. Also, you will very often find it impossible to employ an experienced staff that has used the same approach for improving production in the office area. With several disciplines, you then would need to choose one to be the principal one in your firm, and this could easily result in some resentment between members of your newly created staff. With this in mind, this alternate would not be in your best interest in the long range.

Hiring some key staff with previous office control experience and using them to develop the additional staff from within to carry out your office control program can be very successful. The key to success is making sure of the background of the individual or individuals employed from outside. You must make sure these personnel have both management and training capability. Of utmost importance, however, is management capability, as very often part of the training needs can be leased from outside sources. This alternate can be successful provided you find the right personnel to spearhead it.

Selecting your office control staff from within and using an outside consultant to assist in developing this staff and your program is by far the most widely used. Programs handled in this manner have been both succesful and unsuccessful. The real key to success lies in the clout this staff has within your firm and how good the consultant does his job. By clout we mean support from a key management person on a day-to-day basis as well as the full support of management in the program's objectives. With the proper clout and assistance from the consultant, this approach should be a success. However, if either is lacking, the program will falter.

Using an outside consultant to carry out your entire program is the poorest alternate of all, as your program will die when the consultant leaves. This should never be considered as a means of carrying out an office control program.

Our recommendations for carrying out a successful office control program would be:

1.  To create as much of your office control staff as feasible from within—you may wish to hire an experienced person to head up the staff; and
2.  To utilize outside consultants for training of staff and providing limited guidance in the use of the disciplines taught.

By handling your program in this manner you will provide your own staff with an opportunity to expand their abilities by being trained and assisted by individuals with a wide variety of experiences in the disciplines needed in your program.

## Keeping Your Program Active

Your firm has decided to establish an office productivity improvement program, you have management's full support, and you have everything under way. The program as such is progressing; however, your office improvement staff encounters a department head who has established a program and wants no part of the new program. In fact, this person flatly refused to cooperate with your office improvement staff. All efforts by the officer in charge of the program have been to no avail. How do we handle the situation?

The best method of handling such situations is to have established a vehicle for dealing with this in the very beginning of your program. The best vehicle for handling such situations is a Steering Committee consisting of a top officer of your firm, the head of Personnel, several department heads who truly support the program, and the head of your office improvement group. A top officer of your firm is normally the chairman of this Steering Committee.

The Steering Committee will meet monthly during the implementation of your program to:

1. Review the progress of the program;
2. Discuss any difficulties encountered and make recommendations on how the difficulties should be overcome; and
3. Review all requests for additional staff and approve or disapprove the requests.

In the case of the department head who refused to cooperate, the Steering Committee would review the situation fully with the department head and then decide what action should be taken. The action decided on by the Steering Committee would then be fully explained to both the department head and head of the office improvement staff. The decision of the Steering Committee would be final.

When your office productivity improvement program is on stream and running smoothly, the Steering Committee will need to meet only on an as-needed basis. Their major function will be to review requests for staff increases, review the program's effectiveness, and consider the advisability of new or improved methods, equipment, or techniques for further improving overall office activity. We would recommend, as a minimum, at least one meeting every three months for this purpose. All needed information for the Steering Committee's decisions would be prepared by the office productivity improvement group.

## chapter five

# Introducing Your Office Improvement Program

As SOON AS THE PLANS for your office improvement program are completed, you must then inform all members of your firm of the program and its purpose. This is the only way your program will be a success. The less mystery related to an office improvement program, the better its chances of success.

From our discussion to date, the purpose of an office improvement program is obviously to improve productivity and costs. However, to be successful, it must not result in employees losing their jobs. In normal times, attrition will eventually make possible any staff reductions needed. True, in some areas, attrition may result in prolonging potential benefits. Even so, taking your time will result in better overall morale and a healthier program in the long run. Even if attrition is slow, increased business will often serve the same end result.

Now the question arises in your mind, "How do I announce the purpose of an office improvement program without inferring directly or indirectly that employees will lose their jobs?" It is not difficult, as all you have to say is, "Our office improvement program is to improve the utilization of our most important asset—our employees—without jeopardizing the jobs of any of our employees." Later on when an employee leaves and you do not replace that employee, you have lived up to exactly what you said you would do. By not replacing the employee, you did not jeopardize any of the remaining employees.

The methods by which an office improvement program are announced vary from firm to firm. Most announcements are a variation of the following three:

1. Presentations of the program at normally scheduled meetings between various levels of management, followed by first-line supervision conducting meetings with their employees—this is known as the meeting approach.
2. Presentations of the program at normally scheduled meetings between various levels of management and utilizing either a house organ or letter to all employees to formally present the program—this is known as the meeting/confirmation approach.
3. Presentations of the program at top management meetings and utilizing either a house organ or letter to all employees to formally present the program—this is known as the management approach.

The pros and cons of each of these approaches will now be discussed.

## Meeting Approach

The meeting approach to announcing an office improvement program will vary from firm to firm. For our discussion we will consider a firm consisting of a top management group with each member of this group being over several departments and each department including several sections. With this in mind we will briefly discuss how the meeting approach would function.

The announcement of the program would be made and discussed in the top management group. The announcement and discussion very often end up in the form of minutes of the meeting in which the announcement occurred. Using these minutes and their own thoughts concerning the program, area managers each announce the program to the department managers within their area of responsibility. More than likely, no minutes will be made of these meetings. The department managers in turn hold meetings and announce the program to their section supervisors. The section supervisors then hold meetings with their employees and announce the program.

The personal contact of various levels of management with their employees in this approach is a real plus. However, this plus can and often does result in just the opposite unless there is some way to make sure each presentation covers the announcement of the program in a similar manner. Unfortunately, as the announcement is passed by word of mouth from one level of management to another, the true meaning of the program could easily be lost.

If you have ever experienced what can happen to a story when it is related from person to person and finally gets back to the originator, you will understand what can happen. Therefore, if this method of announcing a program is used, the only way to make sure all personnel receive the same message is to have one person assigned the responsibility of making the announcement in each meeting. This could be difficult to do.

## Meeting/Confirmation Approach

This approach consists of the same steps as previously discussed except following the meetings an announcement of the program is made in writing. The announcement can be published in a house organ or in a letter addressed to all employees from either the chairman or president of the firm.

Figure 5-1 is a typical letter announcement made by a firm to all members of its staff. Figure 5-2 is typical of an announcement made through a house organ. In some instances both are done following announcement meetings at all levels.

In both of these examples you will note that the office productivity improvement program has been given a name. This is not unusual, and we will discuss this briefly later in this chapter.

This method of introducing an office improvement program can be very successful provided the introductions made in meetings are consistent with the written announcement. As in the meeting approach, you must make sure the presentations in meetings at each level of the firm convey the true objectives of the program.

Dear Employee:

In today's fast-paced world, adaptability is very important. To be able to meet the changing needs of our customers, we must keep up with new methods and procedures. However, to analyze the value of any new methods, we need a thorough knowledge of our present systems so that we can make meaningful comparisons.

Figure 5-1 (Cont. on following page.)

We need information on how our work is done, how long it takes to perform a job, and where we can make improvements. Only with such information can we intelligently make the decisions necessary for _____ to maintain its competitive position in the insurance industry. Under the direction of the Controller's Department, we are introducing a program called _____ _____ which will develop these needed information tools. There are many things we intend to accomplish through this program, but _____ is designed primarily to provide ways of planning, scheduling, and controlling our work.

What the _____ program will do is put an analyst in the department to interview you and to learn about your work. By performing this study the analyst will bring to light many small and large problems you've noticed while doing your job. Then the analyst will devote his/her full attention to solving those problems. The analyst will also help you determine how long it should take to do each job. This will serve as a goal for each of us and as a tool for supervisors and managers to use in scheduling work loads.

What the _____ program will not do is reduce our need for capable employees. It is important to realize that we are not talking about people and the way they do their work. Rather, we are talking about procedures and the way we have people doing their work. Our greatest asset is our people, and without the energy, ability, and pride you bring to work each day nothing could be accomplished. Thus, we constantly endeavor to provide the best working conditions possible. The _____ program will ensure you of getting the recognition you deserve and by improving methods will remove the irritating details and problems which prevent you from working as effectively as possible.

In order for all this to happen, the _____ program needs you. It needs your cooperation and assistance. You are the expert at how your job is being done, so you're in the best position to tell the analyst how improvement can be made. With your knowledge of your job and the analyst's ability to spend the time necessary to devise your job solutions, we most certainly can achieve _____ _____.

Sincerely,

_____

President

Figure 5-1 (cont.)

## HAPPENINGS WITHIN OUR FIRM

On October 12, we will start our Productivity Improvement Program. The program will involve training of five of our staff members in the basic techniques that will be used by our staff. Assisting in the training phase will be Frank Pass of the Serge A. Birn Company.

Our productivity improvement staff will consist of John Smith from Customer Service, Joan Jones from Central Files, Ellen Williams from Billing, Jim Watterson from Internal Audit, and a newcomer to our firm—George Bailey. George Bailey headed up the productivity improvement program for First National Bank before joining our firm last month.

All of you will have the opportunity to meet members of this group in the next few months. They will be discussing with you the details relating to your job and ideas you may have for improving it. Your assistance will be the key to making this program a success.

The purpose of the program is to improve the utilization of our staff as opposed to reducing staff. To continue to grow, we must provide the best services possible to our customers at prices equal to or below our competitors.

Figure 5-2

# Management Approach

What we have chosen to call the management approach is the introduction used by most firms. That is, discussions of the program and its purpose are made at top management and department manager level meetings and confirmed to all levels through a letter or an article in the house organ.

Once the letter or article is out, informal meetings can be scheduled to discuss questions related to the program. However, if the announcement is properly prepared, these provide merely a clarification of wording. This approach is normally the best, as everyone receives the announcement in the same manner.

## Program Names

Establishing an acronym for a program name eliminates the necessity of always referring to the office productivity improvement program. In fact, PIP (Productivity Improvement Program) could be used, but it may prove too amusing.

Some of the acronyms used and their meanings are:

| | |
|---|---|
| ACT | Analysis Controls Techniques |
| MOD | Modern Operations Design |
| PEP | Performance Evaluation Program |
| SMART | Supervisors Methods Analysis and Rating Technique |
| STEP | Supervisory Techniques (for) Effective Planning |
| SWAP | Supervisors Work Appreciation Program |

No matter what the acronym is, the true meaning of the program must always be a part of your day-to-day operations to be a success.

## chapter six

# Selecting Program Personnel and Pilot Areas

THE MOST SUCCESSFUL OFFICE productivity improvement programs are those carried out by personnel selected from within. This is understandable, as properly selected personnel already know how the firm operates and where needed information can be located. However, when personnel are selected from within, they must be properly trained in the disciplines that will be utilized to improve productivity.

This training can best be obtained through the use of consultants who specialize in the desired disciplines, but when selecting the consultant be sure that continued training is available on either a continuous basis in a public training center or through media your firm can utilize internally. Beware of training you do internally that is only available by your firm having a qualified instructor to conduct the training. From a prestige point of view it is good to have a qualified instructor, but from an economical point of view this is often very costly.

Both classroom and on-the-job training are needed to develop an office productivity staff. The formal classroom training introduces your personnel to the principles of the disciplines selected and provides some practice opportunity in utilizing these principles to improve productivity. After the classroom training is completed, then training or guidance is needed to provide your personnel with firsthand experience in applying the disciplines to improve office productivity.

To conduct the classroom training you must select the personnel to be assigned the responsibility of carrying out the productivity improvement program.

To provide on-the-job training, pilot areas for implementing the disciplines must be selected. The personnel who conduct productivity improvement programs are called by various titles, with the word "analyst" normally a part of the title. For our discussions we will refer to them as "productivity improvement analysts" or simple "analysts."

We will now discuss the selection of analysts and follow with the discussion of pilot areas.

## Selection of Analysts

In selecting the analysts for your office productivity improvement program, you must decide at the outset where the productivity improvement group will report and how they are to function within your organization. If they are to have the necessary clout to truly implement a sound productivity improvement program and then maintain the program as an ongoing way of life, they should report directly to an officer of your firm who has influence throughout your organization. Whether this is the head of operations, finance, or services does not really matter provided the support and clout are behind the program.

Next, you must decide who will ultimately manage the day-to-day activities of the productivity improvement group. Obviously, it will not be the officer responsible for the group. The best approach is the selection of some promising younger management person who fully realizes and supports improving productivity. The other alternative is to find such a person from outside your organization but this will not serve to provide growth from within.

The person selected to manage the productivity improvement group must be a person who has demonstrated:

1. The ability to sell ideas to others;
2. The ability to be a good listener as well as talker and to give proper consideration to pertinent points raised in discussion;
3. The ability to some degree to delegate responsibility and needed authority; and
4. The intelligence to know when to present problems to a superior and not to run to that person each time some simple problem is encountered.

True, this enumerates the abilities required of a top grade manager. After all, if it is to be successful, your productivity improvement program needs good management.

Once you have selected the manager, then you are in the position of selecting analysts. You should involve your manager in this selection. Before making the selection you should consider what the ultimate growth potential of the analysts will be within your organization. Several alternates are available; however, we will discuss only three. These are:

1. Using the productivity improvement group as a training ground for future managers;
2. Using the productivity improvement group as a training ground for internal service functions; or
3. Using the productivity improvement group as an entity within itself.

Each of these has advantages and disadvantages, and each will now be discussed.

If you decide to use the productivity improvement group as a training ground for future managers, you must decide at the outset that future managers each will spend at least one year in the group. This will make their time worthwhile in the productivity improvement group and will provide an excellent insight into the overall workings of your firm. It will provide them with an understanding of how operations actually function from one area to another which would take years to obtain through other means. The disadvantage of this alternate is that your productivity improvement group will constantly turn over and require retraining at least annually. Naturally, once the productivity improvement group has been in operation for at least one year, then an overlap of management trainees could be set up.

Using the productivity improvement group as a training ground for internal service functions, such as systems analysis, internal auditing, etc., would definitely give each member an understanding of the importance of productivity. However, some of the excellent traits needed for pure systems analysis work or internal auditing would be poor traits for handling productivity improvement. Thus, this alternate would need careful selection and handling of personnel. The disadvantage of this alternate is that again it could result in constant turnover of personnel, necessitating constant training of new personnel.

Using the productivity improvement group as an entity within itself would result in a stable group for a period of time. It would also result in less expense in training of personnel. In the long run you would find that many of the personnel would become dissatisfied and look for other opportunities within or outside your firm. Some personnel would be satisfied in this work, but some 40 to 50 percent of the staff would eventually either leave or move to other positions within the firm.

In reality your best bet is to have a combination of professional productivity improvement analysts and management trainees make up your productivity improvement group. Selecting the management trainees should follow your normal methods. We will now direct our attention to the selection of the potential professional analysts.

Within your present organization you no doubt have many employees who would welcome the opportunity to develop a better profession than that of a typist, clerk, etc. These employees usually have better than normal intelligence, a high school education or possibly as much as two years of college training, an ability to talk with others and sell their ideas to others, and the inherent ability to get along well with others.

Immediately, you are probably saying that these are the abilities we look for in management trainees. True, but with one important exception—most firms look for a minimum of a bachelor's degree with a desire to attain a master's. In our example we omitted the degree and the desire for higher degrees. This does not, however, eliminate the fact that once selected and given the opportunity, the analysts will not have the desire to complete a degree and even go for advanced degrees. If so, and they have the ability, you should encourage and assist them, as it is an investment that could pay off in your firm's growth.

The real clue in selecting the potential professional analysts is to make sure the educational level of the candidates or true growth desire is not higher than that of the positions to be filled. If they aspire to be tomorrow's managers, it is very doubtful that they will succeed as professional analysts.

Good professional productivity improvement analysts have the ability to listen carefully, determine the meaningful data from the information gathered, and put the data to work to create a program that will improve productivity. Naturally, once the program is developed, they must also have the ability to explain and sell it. With proper assistance from a good manager and proper training, this latter quality should develop.

## Selecting Pilot Areas

In the beginning of a productivity improvement program, the pilot areas must meet two important criteria. They should be:

1. Areas where management truly supports the productivity improvement program; and
2. Areas where the overall work performed is not highly technical and complicated.

Careful selection of pilot areas is very important to the overall success of your productivity improvement program.

These areas will serve as a showcase to assist in selling all other areas of your firm on the program benefits. They will also serve as the on-the-job training for your analysts and provide them with the confidence needed to tackle future problems of a sound productivity program.

In most firms you will find departments where management has always made an effort to improve operations to better utilize employees. These departments are normally good areas to approach to select areas for your pilot implementation of the productivity improvement program. True, you may not make earth shattering improvements in these areas, but of more importance, you will probably get excellent cooperation. Cooperation and support of the program in the beginning are far more important than outstanding results. They will provide confidence for the analysts and establish a sound basis on which your program can grow.

Make sure that the pilot areas are not too large in relation to the number of employees and jobs performed. Introducing newly trained analysts to large areas with a wide variety of jobs can result in a discouraging and negative experience for the analysts. After all, they are just learning how to properly apply the techniques they have been taught. Since they will be slow in the beginning, they need areas that are compatible in size so they can see their progress. Areas consisting of 10 to no more than 12 employees performing similar jobs are normally best in the beginning for an analyst to tackle.

It is not absolutely necessary to make a survey of the proposed pilot areas before starting the productivity improvement program, but it can be useful to ensure success. If time permits, interview the supervisors of the proposed pilot areas and find out what kind of work is performed; how many people are performing the work; what jobs are done daily, weekly, and monthly; and how work is received and disposed of after completion.

For example, a survey is made of three areas with the following results:

| Item | Area A | Area B | Area C |
|---|---|---|---|
| Kind of work | Routine posting and checking of applications | Reviewing and approving applications | Entering payments and balancing totals |
| How many people | 10 | 15 | 12 |
| Jobs—Daily | 20 | 10 | 25 |
| Jobs—Weekly | 2 | 12 | 5 |
| Jobs—Monthly | 2 | 6 | 3 |
| Jobs received | in batches of 100 | sporadically throughout day | in batches of 200 |
| Jobs disposed of | in batches of 100 | sporadically throughout day | in batches of 200 |

The chances are that Areas A and C will serve as good pilot areas. Area B would probably cause problems for a new analyst until he or she gained experience. Naturally, a more detailed survey would result in even more information for proper selection.

## Summary

We have discussed in this chapter how your productivity group is to be structured, the selection of personnel for the productivity group, and selection of a pilot area in which to begin the productivity improvement program. An important item that has not been covered is how many analysts are needed to implement the program? Also, once it is implemented, how many analysts are needed maintain it? Both answers are essential to your program plans.

First, the number of analysts needed to implement an office productivity improvement program will depend on:

1. The number of disciplines to be included in your program for improving productivity; and
2. How fast you wish the implementation of the program to progress.

An ideal office productivity improvement program will consist of both the behavioral science and industrial engineering disciplines. That is, jobs will be analyzed and developed so they will provide challenge to motivate the employees. These jobs will then be measured so the employees will have the needed goals to attain. This complete program will obviously take longer than one involving either just the behavioral science or the industrial engineering discipline.

The approximate time requirements for the ideal program with the behavioral science and industrial engineering disciplines being utilized together can be calculated using the following formula:

Total Man-days = $45 + 6.0\,D + 1.5\,S + .75\,J + 2.25\,E$

*Legend*

$D$ = Total No. of Departments in program
$S$ = Total No. of Sections in program

J = Total No. of Job Titles to be covered

E = Total No. of Employees to be covered.

If we had 30 departments, 60 sections, 50 job titles, and 300 employees to be included in our program, then the total man-days required would be:

Total Man-Days = 45 + 6.0 (30) + 1.5 (60) + .75 (50) + 2.25 (300) = 45 + 180 + 90 + 37.5 + 675 = 1027.5.

The 1027.5 man-days could then be converted to number of analysts. The actual working days in a year are approximately 225 when vacation, holidays, sick leave, etc., are removed from the total of 260 available work days per year. So if we desire to complete our productivity improvement program in two years, then we would divide 1027.5 by 2 (225), which would result in 2.28 analysts being needed. In reality, this would be the manager of productivity improvement plus two analysts. In a new program we would recommend starting with the manager and three analysts in order to develop two good analysts.

If you selected to use only one discipline for your productivity improvement program, the industrial engineering discipline, then the approximate man-days required could be developed from the following formula:

Total Man-Days = 30 + 4.0 D + 1.0 S + .50 J + 1.50E.

Using the same figures as for the previous formula, this would result in 685 man-days. Completing the program in two years would require 1.52 analysts or the manager plus two analysts in the beginning.

The approximate time formulae presented to date deal with the handling of the industrial engineering (measurement of work) manually. If the computer-aided work measurement system is used, then these formulae will be as follows:

*Disciplines Included*

Behavioral Science and Industrial Engineering

Total Man-Days = $45 + 6.0\,D + 1.5\,S + .75\,K + 1.6875\,E$

Industrial Engineering only

Total Man-Days = $30 + 4.0\,D + 1.0\,S + .50\,J + 1.125\,E.$

You will note that it changes only the man-days per employee, as all other time is devoted to gathering information and selling the program.

Using the computer-aided man-day formulae and recalculating our previous examples result in 858.75 man-days or 1.91 analysts being needed for implementing the behavioral science and industrial engineering disciplined program in two years. For the industrial engineering program only, it results in 572.5 man-days or 1.27 analysts to complete the program in two years. As you can see, the computer does not save a tremendous amount of time in the implementation phase, as the computer cannot gather information, talk to management and employees, and generally sell both management and employees. Where the computer aids is in maintenance of your program, which we discuss in detail in a later chapter.

## chapter seven

# Starting the Productivity Improvement Program

AS HAS BEEN STATED PREVIOUSLY, the ideal office productivity improvement program consists of redesigning jobs so they motivate employees (behavioral science) and measuring jobs to provide goals for employees and management (industrial engineering). Even though the author has a sincere and deep appreciation for the behavioral science portion of the ideal program, we will not incude this portion in this text. Instead, we will approach our discussion with the assumption that this is a part of the program and is taking place concurrently with measurement.

It should be stated that we will start our discussion based on the premise that the analysts have been properly trained in the disciplines needed. Incidentally, this basic training requires approximately two weeks (80 hours) for a sound work measurement approach and one week (40 hours) for the basics of Job Design for Motivation. In other words, either two or three weeks of classroom training have been completed by your analysts.

The 10 steps in making a study are outlined in Figure 7-1, but let's talk about each step briefly.

**1. Assign analyst to department.**   The selection of an analyst to be assigned to a particular department should take into consideration

- Degree of difficulty
- Personality
- Interest and temperament

### OUTLINE OF THE WORK MEASUREMENT STUDY

1. Assign analyst to department
2. First presentation to employees
    A. Purpose of study
    B. How study is conducted
    C. Question and answer period
3. First interview with employees
    A. What tasks are performed
    B. Forms used
    C. Machines used
    D. Reports prepared
    E. How the work flows
4. Prepare task lists and work distribution chart
5. Second interview with employees
    A. How tasks are performed (method)
    B. How often tasks are performed (frequency)
    C. Observe task being performed
    D. Write Task Description
6. Discuss Task Description with supervisor
7. Develop standards
8. Establish work counts
9. Second presentation to employees
    A. Purpose of office measurement program
    B. How the program works
    C. How performances are calculated
    D. Discussion of tasks
    E. Question and answer period
10. Installation

Figure 7-1

The degree of difficulty of the work to be measured is an important factor only immediately following the training course. Some analysts should be given an easy-to-measure unit as a first assignment so they can gain confidence in the technique. Other analysts readily accept the techniques during the training course and look to the more difficult-to-measure work as an interesting challenge.

Matching the personality of the analyst with that of the supervisor is another factor. Consider which analyst would most likely get along well with the particular unit supervisor.

Finally, the interest and temperament of the analyst should be considered. If the analyst is detail-minded, then a keypunch department, proof machine department, or typing department would be good. The highly repetitive operations require a great deal of attention to detail. Work that is fairly routine, but not repetitive, does not require such attention to detail.

**2. First presentation to employees.**   Schedule a presentation to the employees in the department. The supervisor should introduce the analyst who, in turn, will explain the purpose of the study, how it will be conducted, and how the employees will be affected. Figure 7-2 is an example of such a presentation. Employees should be given an opportunity to ask questions at the conclusion of the presentation.

### PRESENTATION TO EMPLOYEES PRIOR TO START OF WORK MEASUREMENT STUDY

I am _____ from the Office Productivity Improvement Department. I will be visiting with each of you for the next few weeks to discuss your jobs. These discussions will be to determine the work you do, how you perform the work, and to determine if any improvements can be made. Since you know your job better than anyone else, your ideas will be very important in possible improvements of how the work is done.

Figure 7-2 (Cont. on following page.)

As you know, for our Company to be successful, it must stay competitive. We must also provide better service to our customers than our competitors, so it is important that we know how much our services cost and attempt to improve both the quality and cost of these services.

To accomplish this our firm has started the _____ _____ Program. This program will be installed in all departments of our firm. The true input to improving our quality of service and cost is each of you. You will provide the information upon which the program will be based.

I will discuss with each of you the various jobs that you perform. These jobs are called tasks, and I will ask you to explain all details concerning each task you perform. I will also appreciate any recommendations each of you has for improving the way tasks are handled.

From the information you furnish, we will prepare a Task Description of each task for either the way it is being performed or the way it should be performed. These task descriptions will then be reviewed with your supervisor who may wish to review them with you.

After the review by your supervisor and his or her approval of the task descriptions, I will then use the task descriptions to establish a standard for doing each task. The standards will be established using predetermined times for each element of work required to perform the task. The total of these times, with an allowance for your personal needs, short interruptions, and normal coffee breaks, will result in a standard for each task.

When the standards are developed for all of the tasks in your area, our Company will then know:

- How much each task costs,
- How many tasks can be handled per day by each person,
- How many people are needed in each department to handle the work load requirements, and
- How well each employee is doing his or her job.

This will provide us with a sound means of controlling our costs to remain competitive.

It should be pointed out that the purpose of this program is not to reduce staff but to better utilize the staff we have. Therefore, you do not need to worry about losing your job as a result of this program.

I look forward to working with each of you and would be happy to answer any questions you may have.

Figure 7-2 (cont.)

**3. First interview with employees.** Having obtained the preliminary information about what goes on in a department from the supervisor, the analyst should interview each employee individually to find out exactly what tasks he or she performs. This will usually take about 10 or 15 minutes per employee. Where large groups of employees performing similar tasks are involved, the interviews will be considerably shorter. Regardless of the number of employees, each one should be interviewed.

From the information obtained, the analyst will make a task list, similar to the one found in Figure 7-3, listing the employees' tasks in order of importance. After this is completed, the analyst should find out how the work is received, where it comes from, and where it goes upon completion. At this point "work flow" is being established. Naturally, if flow charts are available, the analyst will make use of them.

Finally, this first interview should elicit information on what forms are used, what office machines are used, and what reports are prepared, so that after all employees are interviewed, the analyst can fill out the forms shown in Figures 7-4, 7-5, and 7-6, and review them with the supervisor.

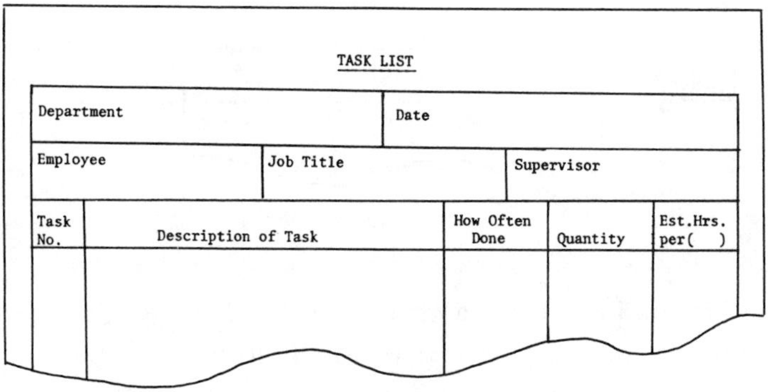

TASK LIST

| | | | | | |
|---|---|---|---|---|---|
| Department | | | Date | | |
| Employee | Job Title | | | Supervisor | |
| Task No. | Description of Task | How Often Done | Quantity | Est.Hrs. per( ) | |

Figure 7-3

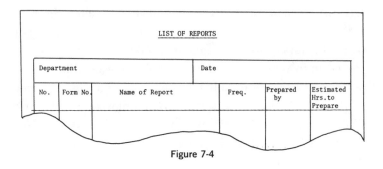

Figure 7-4

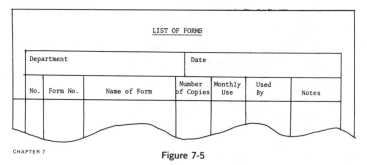

Figure 7-5

Figure 7-6

**4. Prepare Task Lists and Work Distribution Chart.** After every employee has been interviewed and all the Task Lists and flow charts have been completed, the analyst draws up a Work Distribution Chart like the one in Figure 7-7. This chart summarizes all the tasks performed in the unit, the number of employees performing each task, and the beginning of a picture of the operation in terms of work load assignments.

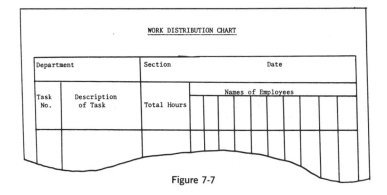

Figure 7-7

The analyst and supervisor should review the Task Lists and Work Distribution Chart to make sure the analyst did not misunderstand or misinterpret the information given by the employees. This review also gives the supervisor a chance to set the analyst straight if inaccuracies exist, and often the supervisor will remember tasks that the employees forgot to mention.

(At this point, even though the work has not been measured, you are generally able to achieve a better distribution of work load just by analyzing the Work Distribution Chart and suggesting that certain procedural changes be made immediately.)

**5. Second interview with employees.**   This is the depth interview in which the analyst concentrates on finding out how each task is performed (method) and how often (frequency). The employee explains the tasks verbally while the analyst takes notes. The analyst will then observe the employee performing the tasks to make certain a complete and accurate picture of each task is obtained.

The importance of the human relations aspect of this part of the study cannot be overemphasized. The analysts should be thoroughly trained in the techniques of interviewing. They should realize that these interviews should be a pleasant experience for the persons being interviewed.

# 64    MCD-MOD-I

<table>
<tr><td colspan="5" align="center">TASK DESCRIPTION</td></tr>
<tr><td>TIME STANDARD</td><td>SYMBOL</td><td></td><td colspan="2">TASK NO.</td></tr>
<tr><td></td><td>DEPARTMENT</td><td></td><td colspan="2">SECTION</td></tr>
<tr><td>TASK</td><td></td><td></td><td colspan="2">DATE EFFECTIVE</td></tr>
<tr><td></td><td></td><td></td><td colspan="2">ANALYST</td></tr>
<tr><td>ITEMS COUNTED</td><td colspan="2">DEPT. AVERAGE PER DAY (TOTAL)</td><td colspan="2">HOW OFTEN DONE</td></tr>
<tr><td colspan="5">EQUIPMENT</td></tr>
<tr><td colspan="5">MATERIALS</td></tr>
<tr><td>APPROVED BY</td><td>DATE APPROVED</td><td>REVISION DATE</td><td colspan="2">REPLACES TASK NO. DATED</td></tr>
</table>

SABCO MCD

Figure 7-8

Make it a point to give all employees in the department a chance to talk about their jobs and ask questions. People are apprehensive about the unknown, and anything you can do to explain things will make the job that much easier in the long run. If 10 people perform a task, interview all 10. Don't cover each minor detail with all of them, but give them every reason to feel that they are an integral part of the study and important to the program as a whole.

Immediately following the interview and observation of the employee doing the work, the analyst writes a narrative Task Description, which describes the best available method for doing each task. An example of a Task Description is found on Figure 7-8.

**6. Discuss Task Description with supervisor.**   The analyst then reviews the step-by-step method and wording of the Task Description with the supervisor, who, after reviewing the description with the employees and being satisfied that the description is complete and accurate, signs the description.

The Task Description serves as a basis for the standard. It describes the conditions that existed at the time the standard was set, the equipment and materials used, and the best available method for doing the task. It is commonly used as a training aid for new employees.

**7. Develop standards.**  From the notes on frequencies obtained in the interview and from the Task Description, the analyst can develop a standard for each task using a predetermined time technique.

**8. Establish work counts.**  The tasks in the unit are set up for reporting based on whether group measurement or individual measurement is used. Individual measurement is usually most desirable since it provides specific performance information on each employee, thus making it possible to pinpoint employees who may need help in attaining proficiency at their jobs.

The reporting controls usually consist of a Daily Production Record and a Daily Time Record for recording off-standard time. These records are maintained by a supervisor or someone designated by the supevisor who is in a position to assign work.

**9. Second presentation to employees.**  Now the supervisor is ready to become even more involved in the program, because it should be his or her job to demonstrate to the employees exactly how they should record their work counts and time distributions.

A sample presentation is given in Figure 7-9. It is advisable to have the analyst present to answer any questions or explain anything that the supervisor may not have the background or training to explain. Basically, however, this is the supervisor's show, and much of the success of the program rests on how well the supervisor motivates the employees to a feeling of enthusiasm about keeping their individual records.

## PRESENTATION TO EMPLOYEES PRIOR TO INSTALLATION OF PROGRAM

For several weeks I have been talking with you about your work. Most of you know the purpose of these interviews. In case there are any misunderstandings about what we are trying to do, we want to discuss with you the purpose of what we call the _____ Program.

With your help I have found out what you do and how often you do it. My studies are now complete. From the information you have given me, I have developed lists of the various tasks you perform and, using data that have been specially developed for your type of work, I have worked up times for performing each task.

Now, what is the purpose of this? It is simply to provide information which will enable you to better utilize your time, to give supervisors something more than guesswork or opinion with which to distribute work, and to tell how well everyone is performing his/her tasks. This means that the supervisor can quickly evaluate progress and tell who needs help in attaining proficiency at his/her job. This is how the _____ Program will work starting this coming Monday.

As has been pointed out, each of your tasks has been assigned time in which it should be performed. From now on we will call this a "standard." Standards represent the time required to perform a task at a normal working pace, and let's call this 100 percent. This 100 percent is not the maximum—it is not perfection. We define 100 percent as "the pace at which an average well-trained employee can work without undue fatigue." Of course, these standards in no way relax the high standards of quality you have always maintained in this department.

Our standards also provide allowances for personal needs such as getting a drink of water or coffee, going to the rest room, and some time for personal conversation. We have also included allowances for setting up your desk in the morning, clearing it off at closing time, getting supplies, sharpening pencils, asking or answering questions, and any small tasks which were not economical to measure directly. These allowances have been tailored to your department's needs and are included in the standards.

In order to determine the amount of acceptable work done by each employee, there is a small amount of record keeping involved. We have established methods of counting the number of items completed by each individual. These counts are to be recorded on a Daily Production Sheet which you will get from your

Figure 7-9 (Cont. on following page)

supervisor each day. In addition, the supervisor will keep on his/ her desk a Daily Signout Sheet. When you have completed your work and have no more work to do, you should report to your supervisor who will either give you more work or ask you to wait for another job. This is very important. You see, the time you spend doing your job is compared with the standard time allowed, the number of items handled multiplied by the standard for each job. In this way we determine how well everyone performs his or her assigned tasks. If you do not tell your supervisor when you have no more work to do, the records will give an entirely incorrect picture.

Suppose for example that you have been assigned enough work to keep you busy for, say, four hours. But by working conscientiously you complete the work in only three and one-half hours. This means that you have exceeded our 100 percent level of performance by 15 percent—an excellent accomplishment for which you should be recognized.

But now, what happens if there is no more work to do? If you report this to your supervisor, he will, as we call it, "take you off standards" by noting that you have finished your job, and he will not show that your are again working "on standards" until more work is available. Your performance will go on record as 115 percent.

However, if you do not report that you have finished, look at what a false picture will result! At the end of the day the record will show that you did (through no fault of yours) only four hours work—but that you took almost eight hours to do it; apparently a performance of 50 percent instead of the 115 percent for which you really should have been recognized.

At this point I would like to make it perfectly clear that an individual does not have to work fast to achieve a good performance. The secret, if you will, is simply to apply yourself continuously to the job and avoid unnecessary delays and excessive interruptions. The quality of your work is of extreme importance. We have built into our standards the necessary time to do a good, quality job.

Let's go over how the work counts will be obtained. (Pass out a copy of the Daily Production Sheet and discuss each task.)

Are there any questions?

Figure 7-9 (Cont.)

**10. Installation.** And so the program is installed. The employees report their times and work counts, the analyst answers any questions, and the supervisor makes sure that everyone is kept busy.

Any bugs are worked out of the record-keeping controls during the first two weeks—normally considered the "dry run."

After the first two weeks, the results are calculated. The analyst meets with the supervisor to discuss and interpret the results. The areas of cost improvement are pinpointed, and the first steps for remedial action are taken.

## chapter eight
# A Typical Employee Interview

ALL OF THE BASIC INFORMATION needed for measuring office work is obtained through interviews with the employees performing the work. During the interview it is very important that the analyst listen carefully to what each employee says and that notes be taken all during the interview.

The interview of the first employee within an area is normally started by the supervisor of that area introducing the analyst to the first employee. Following the introduction by the supervisor, the supervisor leaves the analyst with the employee. The first thing the analyst must do is to make every effort to put the employee at ease so that he or she will talk freely about the work performed. This is normally done by spending the first few minutes talking about trivia—anything that may put the employee at ease. Normally the interview should be a pleasant experience to both the analyst and employee. It furnishes the analyst an opportunity to learn what is done (method) and how often it is done (frequency).

On the other hand, it gives the employee an opportunity to review what he or she does to aid in the overall activity of the firm.

The analyst should always remember that the objective in the interview is not to find out how long it takes to do things. In fact, this should not even be mentioned. The real purpose is to find out what is being done, how it is being done, and how often it is done. Through discussions in the interview, the employee will often suggest better methods for doing the job, and these suggestions plus the notes taken will determine at a later date the best way (method) to do the job in a minimum of time.

## What To Ask

First, the analyst will want a general outline. The first question might simply ask, "What do you do?" and elicit all kinds of replies ranging from "Where do you want me to start?" to a complete documentation of a day's work. Generally, the reply will be somewhere in between.

The job is to get the employee to talk. Once this begins, don't interrupt even if the information is irrelevant or unimportant. Even if it is about personal problems with the supervisor or fellow employees, listen. The employee, not the analyst, is the expert, and the less the analyst acts like an expert, the more will be learned and the more pleasant the interview will be.

As the employee continues, the analyst makes notes of the highlights—points that appear to be major duties. If the interview is properly handled, the analyst will have in these notes 80 percent of the basic job in about 30 minutes.

Here is a vital point worth repeating. Where more than one person is performing the task under study, all those involved must be interviewed. Even though the first conversation gives all the information required, the analyst must talk to *everyone* involved. Failure to do so will ensure the worst kind of human relations.

## A Typical Interview

During an interview an employee will normally describe a number of jobs that he or she performs. These various jobs in office work measurement are referred to as tasks. As you can well imagine, it would require a considerable number of pages in this text to cover a complete typical employee interview. To illustrate a typical interview we will use a hypothetical case covering only one task performed by an employee in an area of our office. The interview will relate to the task of Post Cash Receipts.

To illustrate the interview, we will assume that the introductions are completed and the analyst and Miss Greene are starting to talk about specific tasks. The interview is as follows:

> ANALYST: Miss Greene, you mentioned to me the other day that one of your primary tasks was to "post cash receipts." Would you mind explaining just how this task is done?
>
> MISS GREENE: Not at all. Where do you want me to start?
>
> ANALYST: Just start with how you receive the work and what you do with it until it leaves your desk.
>
> MISS GREENE: A mail clerk drops off an envelope in my "in" basket. I remove the envelope from the "in" basket, remove the checks, and I sort the checks into piles on my desk by the name of the company on the check. Then I further sort each pile into exact sequence. Then I make a listing of the check money amounts on my adding machine. After that I take out my journal, open it to the next open page, write "cash receipts for" and the date at the top of the page; then I post the date of each check, the name of the company, and the amount of each check. I draw a line under the last amount and make another listing of the money amounts—only this time from the journal. Then I compare the total from the first listing with the total from the second listing. If the totals agree, I write it beneath the last amount in the journal. I throw one tape away,

wrap the other around the checks, band them, and put them in my "out" basket where they are picked up by a messenger. And that's it.

While they are talking, the analyst will take notes similar to those on Figure 8-1. After the above discussion, the analyst will ask additional questions as follows:

ANALYST: Fine. Now I'd like to go back and pick up some additional details.

MISS GREENE: OK. What would you like to know?

ANALYST: Is the envelope sealed—and if so, how do you open it?

MISS GREENE: Yes, it is sealed. I use a letter opener, which I keep in my center drawer.

ANALYST: Could you tell me approximately how many checks, on the average, are in an envelope?

MISS GREENE: Well, it varies.

ANALYST: Is it under a hundred?

MISS GREENE: Oh, yes, more like 20 or 30.

ANALYST: Perhaps we can use 25 as the average. Do you have any idea how many envelopes you receive each day?

MISS GREENE: I get one from each office, and we have 24 offices.

ANALYST: Now you said you sort the checks into piles on your desk. How many piles?

MISS GREENE: Five. I have the alphabet broken into five groups. Then I take the first pile or group, which is A–H, and I put them in perfect alphabetical sequence. I do the same with the other piles.

ANALYST: Now, let's take a look at the journal and see if we can get an average number of digits in the check amount. It looks like six is the average to me. What do you think?

MISS GREENE: I think that would be a good figure to use.

ANALYST: Do you always keep the journal in your desk drawer?

MISS GREENE: Yes. It's bulky and I can't keep it on top of my desk.

ANALYST: While we have the journal open, I see you use a bookmark to keep your place in the journal. Good idea. How about helping me determine an average name of company? I need one that has about the average number of words, capital letters, small letters, and punctuation. What do you think of "Allied Tire Co."?

MISS GREENE: Well, I was thinking of "J. R. Griswold, Inc."
ANALYST: I think you're right. It has four capital letters and four punctuations, which seems to be common. You catch on to this very quickly. Now about the ending of the task. You said what you do if the totals agree. What do you do if the totals do not agree?
MISS GREENE: I have to look for my error.
ANALYST: Do you find this happens often?
MISS GREENE: No, I usually balance.
ANALYST: OK, you've been very helpful. After I've written up this task I will come back and have you read it. Thanks.

Preliminary Notes                          Date:  10/1/99

TASK:    Post Cash Receipts
         Miss Edna Greene

1. Receives envelope with checks in "in" basket.
2. Opens envelope, removes checks, sorts into piles by name of company.
3. Sorts checks into alphabetical sequence.
4. Lists amounts on adding machine and totals.
5. Gets journal from desk, opens, writes "cash receipts for" and date.
6. Posts date of check, name of company, amount and draws a line.
7. Lists journal amounts and totals.
8. Compares totals, writes total in journal, bands one tape with checks, discards one tape, and asides banded checks to "out" basket.

Figure 8-1

At this point the analyst has made additional notes, such as Figure 8-2.

With these notes, the analyst is now ready to analyze and measure the task of Post Cash Receipts. However, before doing so, the analyst will have interviewed all employees in the area who post cash receipts.

In the next chapter we will discuss how this task can be measured from the interview notes on Figure 8-2.

Additional Details                                    Date:    10/1/99

TASK:       Post Cash Receipts
            Miss Edna Greene

1. Receives envelope with checks in "in" basket.
      *average 25 at a time*                              *600/day*

2. Opens envelope, removes checks, sorts into piles by name of company.
      *use letter opener from center desk drawer*            *5 piles on desk*

3. Sorts checks into alphabetical sequence.
      *average of 5 per pile*

4. Lists amounts on adding machine and totals.
      *electronic-average 6 digits/check*

5. Gets journal from desk, opens, writes "cash receipts for" and date.
                                                        *10/10/99*

6. Posts date of check, name of company, amount and draws a line.
      *10/10/99*              *J. R. Griswold, Inc.*            *$5,555.55*

7. Lists journal amounts and totals.

                             *2–8 digit numbers*
8. Compares totals, writes total in journal, bands one tape with checks, discards other tape, and asides banded checks to "out" basket.

**Figure 8-2**

## chapter nine

# Measuring a Typical Task

IN THE PREVIOUS CHAPTER we discussed a typical interview concerning the task designated Post Cash Receipts. The notes taken by the analyst during this interview can be used to measure the time required to perform this task at a "fair day's work pace or 100 percent (normal)." The measurement approach we will illustrate for measuring this task is known as Master Clerical Data—MCD.

MCD was the first published clerical work measurement system based on Methods-Time Measurement (MTM), the world's most widely used and respected predetermined time system. Since its introduction in the late 1950s, MCD has been updated through research to keep pace with the ever-changing conditions existing in the office area. The most up-to-date version of MCD, known as MCD-MOD-I, appears in Appendix A. A computer software package has been developed for handling much of the detail needed to properly apply MCD-MOD-I and is known as MCD-MOD-II.

In order for the reader to obtain a feel for what is involved in measuring the task of Post Cash Receipts using the manual and computerized versions of MCD, we will now illustrate each.

## Using MCD-MOD-I Manual Version

In measuring a task either manually or with the computer, the first thing is to break down the task into the meaningful steps required to perform it. This has been done to the notes taken on Figure 8-2, and you will see the results are five steps (A, D, C, D, and E) on Figure 9-1.

Additional Details                                    Date:    10/1/99

TASK:      Post Cash Receipts
           Miss Edna Greene

A.
1. Receives envelope with checks in "in" basket.
      *average 25 at a time*                          *600/day*

2. Opens envelope, removes checks, sorts into piles by name of company.
      *use letter opener from center desk drawer*     *5 piles on desk*

3. Sorts checks into alphabetical sequence.
      *average of 5 per pile*

B.
4. Lists amounts on adding machine and totals.
      *electronic-average 6 digits/check*

C.
5. Gets journal from desk, opens, writes "cash receipts for" and date.                              *10/10/99*

6. Posts date of check, name of company, amount and draws a line.
      *10/10/99*           *J. R. Griswold, Inc.*           *$5,555.55*

D.
7. Lists journal amounts and totals.

E.
      *2–8 digit numbers*
8. Compares totals, writes total in journal, bands one tape with checks, discards other tape, and asides banded checks to "out" basket.

Figure 9-1

From Figure 9-1, the analyst would write up a narrative task description of Post Cash Receipts similar to Figure 9-2. This task description is then reviewed with the supervisor of the area where Post Cash Receipts is performed. After the review and approval by supervision, it is then used to measure each step of the task.

Figures 9-3, 9-4, 9-5, 9-6, and 9-7 are the MCD-MOD-I analyses and times for each of these steps. So that you can better understand each of these, we have written a description by each in more detail than is normally required. You can find the values for each in Appendix A.

Once the analysis of each step is completed, then the steps are summarized on a Task Summary (Figure 9-8) and the time per check developed. You will note on Figure 9-8 that the total of each step has a frequency of 1/25. This is due to the fact that we wanted the standard to be in hours per check. You will also see on Figure 9-8 that an allowance of 15 percent has been used to develop the standard. This could vary from firm to firm.

The standard developed on Figure 9-8 would then be placed on the Task Description (Figure 9-2) with the result being Figure 9-9. This would then be used to control this task.

## Using MCD-MOD-II Computer Version

To measure the task of Post Cash Receipts using the computer software, known as MCD-MOD-II, we need only use Figure 9-1 to enter pertinent information via a CRT. However, rather than simulate a CRT on-line, we will illustrate how this would be done through data entry. This, in turn, will furnish us with a comparison of manual versus computer paperwork requirements.

Figure 9-10 would be prepared to enter the information contained on the top of Figure 9-2 (Task Description). You will note at the bottom of Figure 9-10 there is a place to enter allowance (%). If nothing is entered, the program automatic-

## TASK DESCRIPTION

| TIME STANDARD | SYMBOL PCR | | TASK NO. 1 |
|---|---|---|---|
| | DEPARTMENT Accounting | | SECTION Processing |
| TASK Post Cash Receipts | | | DATE EFFECTIVE 12-1-99 |
| | | | ANALYST CLN |
| ITEMS COUNTED Checks | DEPT. AVERAGE PER DAY (TOTAL) 600 | | HOW OFTEN DONE once per check |
| EQUIPMENT Desk, electronic printing calculator,"in" and "out" baskets & letter opener | | | |
| MATERIALS Checks, journal, envelopes, pen & rubber bands | | | |
| APPROVED BY HWN | DATE APPROVED 11/28/99 | REVISION DATE | REPLACES TASK NO. DATED |

SABCO MCD

STEP A:    RECEIVE AND SORT CHECKS

Get envelope containing checks from "in" basket. Open envelope with letter opener, remove checks, and aside envelope. Sort checks (25) into five piles by company name. Then sort checks into alphabetical order.

STEP B:    ADD UP CHECKS ON CALCULATOR

Enter amount of each check on calculator, total all amounts, tear off tape, and aside tape on desk.

STEP C:    POST CHECKS IN JOURNAL

Get journal from desk drawer, place in center of desk, and open to blank page. Get pen and write cash receipts for date posted on top of page. Post date of each check, name of company, and amount on check. Draw line under last amount posted.

STEP D:    ADD AMOUNTS POSTED

Enter each amount posted on journal in calculator and total. Tear tape from calculator.

STEP E:    WRAP-UP

Get tape from total of checks, compare with that of journal total. If totals are the same, post total in journal and aside one tape in wastebasket. Aside pen, close journal and aside in drawer. Align checks, place tape on checks, band checks and tape, and aside to "out" basket.

Figure 9-2

| | CLERICAL METHODS | | | | | |
|---|---|---|---|---|---|---|
| Sheet __1__ of __5__ | ANALYSIS SHEET | | | Task No. PCR-1 | | |

Department ___Accounting___  Section ___Processing___

Task ___Post Cash Receipts___  Step _A. Receive and Sort Checks_

Date _10/8/99_  Analyst ___CLN___  Supervisor ___HWN___

| MCD CODE | DESCRIPTION | Var. | Work Units | Freq. | Total Units | Seq. No. |
|---|---|---|---|---|---|---|
| GST | Get envelope and move to desk | Batch | 36 | 1 | 36 | |
| ODD | Open and later close drawer | " | 62 | 1 | 62 | |
| MOSU01 | Open envelope, remove checks, and | | | | | |
| | aside envelope | " | 132 | 1 | 132 | |
| GAT | Aside letter opener | " | 15 | 1 | 15 | |
| ASG | Sort checks into piles | Check | 47 | 25 | 1,175 | |
| ASA-01 | Sort checks alphabetically | " | 72 | 25 | 1,800 | |
| | | | | | | |
| | | | | | | |
| | | | | | | |
| | | | | | | |
| | | | | | | |
| | | | | | | |
| | | | | | | |
| | | | | | | |
| | | | | | | |
| | | | | | | |
| | | | | | | |
| | | | | | | |
| | | | | | | |
| | | | | | | |
| | | | | | | |
| | | | | | | |

| CODE | Identification | Frequencies | Total Work Units | | 3,220 | |
|---|---|---|---|---|---|---|
| | | | | | | |
| | | | | | | |
| | | | | | | |
| | | | | | | |

Figure 9-3

| | CLERICAL METHODS ANALYSIS SHEET | | | | | | |
|---|---|---|---|---|---|---|---|

Sheet __2__ of __5__    Task No. __PCR-1__

Department __Accounting__    Section __Processing__

Task __Post Cash Receipts__    Step __B.__ __Add Up Checks on Calculator__

Date __10/8/99__ Analyst __CLN__    Supervisor __HWN__

| MCD CODE | DESCRIPTION | Var. | Work Units | Freq. | Total Units | Seq. No. |
|---|---|---|---|---|---|---|
| CEAP01 | Clear and total calculator | Batch | 21 | 1 | 21 | |
| CEAP03 | Enter each check | Check | 29 | 25 | 725 | |
| HSF | Flip checks during entry | " | 23 | 25 | 575 | |
| GGM | Adding machine tape | Batch | 18 | 1 | 18 | |
| HTN | Tear off tape | " | 23 | 1 | 23 | |
| GAT | Aside to desk | " | 15 | 1 | 15 | |
| | | | | | | |
| | | | | | | |
| | | | | | | |
| | | | | | | |
| | | | | | | |
| | | | | | | |
| | | | | | | |
| | | | | | | |
| | | | | | | |
| | | | | | | |
| | | | | | | |
| | | | | | | |
| | | | | | | |
| | | | | | | |
| | | | | | | |
| | | | | | | |

| CODE | Identification | Frequencies | Total Work Units | | 1,377 | |
|---|---|---|---|---|---|---|
| | | | | | | |
| | | | | | | |
| | | | | | | |

Serge A. Birn Company

Figure 9-4

| | CLERICAL METHODS ANALYSIS SHEET | | | | | | |
|---|---|---|---|---|---|---|---|
| Sheet __3__ of __5__ | | | Task No. PCR-1 | | | | |
| Department __Accounting__ | | Section __Processing__ | | | | | |
| Task __Post Cash Receipts__ | | Step _C._ __Post Checks in Journal__ | | | | | |
| Date __10/8/99__ Analyst __CLN__ | | Supervisor __HWN__ | | | | | |

| MCD CODE | DESCRIPTION | Var. | Work Units | Freq. | Total Units | Seq. No. |
|---|---|---|---|---|---|---|
| ODD | Open and close desk drawer | Batch | 62 | 1 | 62 | |
| GBT | Journal to desk | " | 46 | 1 | 46 | |
| OBC01 | Open and later close journal | " | 48 | 1 | 48 | |
| LPBE | Locate blank journal page | " | 134 | 1 | 134 | |
| GMT | Pen and move to journal | " | 33 | 1 | 33 | |
| WSW01 | Write "cash receipts for" | " | 78 | 3 | 234 | |
| WSD02 | Write date 10/10/99 | " | 130 | 1 | 130 | |
| GBT | Turn checks over | " | 46 | 1 | 46 | |
| PDN | Post date on check | Check | 144 | 25 | 3,600 | |
| PAN | Post name of firm | " | 359 | 25 | 8,975 | |
| PNA | Post amount of check | " | 129 | 25 | 3,225 | |
| WP | Draw line under last amount | Batch | 15 | 1 | 15 | |

| CODE | Identification | Frequencies | Total Work Units | 16,548 |
|---|---|---|---|---|
| | | | | |

© 1972    Serge A. Birn Company    201

Figure 9-5

| Sheet 4 of 5 | | CLERICAL METHODS ANALYSIS SHEET | | | | Task No. PCR-1 | | |
|---|---|---|---|---|---|---|---|---|
| Department Accounting | | | Section Processing | | | | | |
| Task Post Cash Receipts | | | Step D. Add Amounts Posted | | | | | |
| Date 10/8/99 Analyst CLN | | | Supervisor HWN | | | | | |

| MCD CODE | DESCRIPTION | Var. | Work Units | Freq. | Total Units | Seq. No. |
|---|---|---|---|---|---|---|
| CEAP01 | Clear and total machine | Batch | 21 | 1 | 21 | |
| CEAP03 | Enter each posted total | " | 29 | 25 | 725 | |
| GGM | Get tape | " | 18 | 1 | 18 | |
| HTN | Tear off tape | " | 23 | 1 | 23 | |
| | | | | | | |
| | | | | | | |
| | | | | | | |
| | | | | | | |
| | | | | | | |
| | | | | | | |
| | | | | | | |
| | | | | | | |
| | | | | | | |
| | | | | | | |
| | | | | | | |
| | | | | | | |
| | | | | | | |
| | | | | | | |
| | | | | | | |
| | | | | | | |
| | | | | | | |
| | | | | | | |

| CODE | Identification | Frequencies | Total Work Units | | 787 |
|---|---|---|---|---|---|
| | | | | | |
| | | | | | |
| | | | | | |
| | | | | | |

Figure 9-6

| Sheet 5 of 5 | CLERICAL METHODS ANALYSIS SHEET | | | Task No. PCR-1 | | |
|---|---|---|---|---|---|---|
| Department Accounting | | Section Processing | | | | |
| Task Post Cash Receipts | | Step E. Wrap-Up | | | | |
| Date 10/8/99 Analyst CLN | | Supervisor HWN | | | | |

| MCD CODE | DESCRIPTION | Var. | Work Units | Freq. | Total Units | Seq. No. |
|---|---|---|---|---|---|---|
| GST | Previous tape to work area | Batch | 36 | 1 | 36 | |
| ERDS | Read totals on tapes | " | 7 | 6 | 42 | |
| EM3 | Move eyes between tapes | " | 3 | 2 | 6 | |
| EDS | Decide if totals are same | " | 11 | 1 | 11 | |
| GAT | Aside tape in wastebasket | " | 15 | 1 | 15 | |
| PNN | Post total to journal | " | 193 | 1 | 193 | |
| GAT | Aside pen and tape | " | 15 | 1 | 15 | |
| ODD | Open and close drawer | " | 62 | 1 | 62 | |
| GBT | Journal to drawer | " | 46 | 1 | 46 | |
| GBT | Checks up from desk | " | 46 | 1 | 46 | |
| HJS01 | Align checks | " | 8 | 3 | 24 | |
| GSH | Tape to checks | " | 41 | 1 | 41 | |
| FRP | Fasten checks and tape with band | " | 129 | 1 | 129 | |
| GAT | Checks to "out" basket | " | 15 | 1 | 15 | |

| CODE | Identification | Frequencies | Total Work Units | 681 |
|---|---|---|---|---|
| | | | | |

1972        Serge A. Birn Company        201

Figure 9-7

| | | Task Code PCR-1 |
|---|---|---|

**TASK SUMMARY SHEET**   Task Code __PCR-1__   Sheet __1__ of __1__

Department ___Accounting___     Section ___Processing___

Job ___Posting Clerk___     Task ___Post Cash Receipts___

Prepared by ___CLN___ Date ___10/8/99___ Approved by ___HWN___

| Step | Description | Time | Freq. | Total |
|---|---|---|---|---|
| A | Receive and sort checks | 3,220 | 1/25 | 129 |
| B | Add checks on calculator | 1,377 | 1/25 | 55 |
| C | Post checks in journal | 16,548 | 1/25 | 662 |
| D | Add amounts posted | 787 | 1/25 | 31 |
| E | Wrap up | 681 | 1/25 | 27 |

Remarks:

| | |
|---|---|
| Total This Sheet | 904 |
| Total Previous Sheet | - |
| TOTAL | 904 |
| 15 % Allowance | 136 |
| Allowed Time | 1,040 |
| Hours / Check | .0104 |
| Pcs./Hour | 96.2 |

© 1975 Serge A. Birn Company     No. 202

Figure 9-8

**TASK DESCRIPTION**

| TIME STANDARD .0104 96.2 checks/hour | SYMBOL PCR | | TASK NO. 1 |
|---|---|---|---|
| | DEPARTMENT Accounting | | SECTION Processing |
| TASK Post Cash Receipts | | | DATE EFFECTIVE 12-1-99 |
| | | | ANALYST CLN |
| ITEMS COUNTED Checks | DEPT. AVERAGE PER DAY (TOTAL) 600 | | HOW OFTEN DONE once per check |
| EQUIPMENT Desk, electronic printing calculator,"in" and "out" baskets & letter opener | | | |
| MATERIALS Checks, journal, envelopes, pen & rubber bands | | | |
| APPROVED BY HWN | DATE APPROVED 11/28/99 | REVISION DATE | REPLACES TASK NO. DATED |

SABCO MCD

*STEP A:*  RECEIVE AND SORT CHECKS

> *Get envelope containing checks from "in" basket. Open envelope with letter opener, remove checks, and aside envelope. Sort checks (25) into five piles by company name. Then sort checks into alphabetical order.*

*STEP B:*  ADD UP CHECKS ON CALCULATOR

> *Enter amount of each check on calculator, total all amounts, tear off tape, and aside tape on desk.*

*STEP C:*  POST CHECKS IN JOURNAL

> *Get journal from desk drawer, place in center of desk, and open to blank page. Get pen and write cash receipts for date posted on top of page. Post date of each check, name of company, and amount on check. Draw line under last amount posted.*

*STEP D:*  ADD AMOUNTS POSTED

> *Enter each amount posted on journal in calculator and total. Tear tape from calculator.*

*STEP E:*  WRAP-UP

> *Get tape from total of checks, compare with that of journal total. If totals are the same, post total in journal and aside one tape in wastebasket. Aside pen, close journal and aside in drawer. Align checks, place tape on checks, band checks and tape, and aside to "out" basket.*

**Figure 9-9**

MCD-MOD II TASK CODING SHEET I

TASK NO. `PCA-1`    REV. NO. ☐    TRANS TYPE ☐    REPORT CODE ☐

TASK NAME `POST CASH RECEIPTS`

INPUT TASK NO. ☐    REV. ☐

HEADING INFORMATION

DEPARTMENT `ACCOUNTING`

SECTION `PROCESSING`

JOB `POSTING CLERK`

ANALYST `GLN`

DATE CODED `10-8-99`

EFFECTIVE DATE `12-1-99`

ITEM COUNTED `CHECKS`

BATCH SIZE `25`

DAILY COUNT `600`

HOW OFTEN DONE `ONCE PER CHECK`

EQUIPMENT [1] `DESK, ELECTRONIC PRINTING CALCULA-`

EQUIPMENT [2] `TOR, OUT AND IN BASKET AND LETTER`

EQUIPMENT [3] `OPENER`

MATERIALS [1] `CHECKS, JOURNAL, ENVELOPES, PEN,`

MATERIALS [2] `AND RUBBER BANDS`

MATERIALS [3]

SUPERSEDES

SUPERSEDED BY

ALLOWANCE (%)

RBL · 01/80                                   PAGE / OF 3

**Figure 9-10**

ally uses 15 percent; however, if an entry is made, the entry will be used.

Figures 9-11 and 9-12 are the entries needed to measure this task. You will note that no entry is made in the "frequency" column when the frequency is 25. This is due to the fact that the program automatically uses the step count when no entry is made under frequency opposite an MCD-MOD-I code. The input that has been prepared will use standard

TASK NO [PCR-II]  REV NO [19]  TRANS TYPE [21]

| STEP | LINE | TITLE/DESCRIPTION/OBJECT | MCD CODE | Step Count | FREQUENCY |
|---|---|---|---|---|---|
| 1 | | RECEIVE AND SORT CHECKS | GST | 25 | / |
| | | ENVELOPE. | ODD | | / |
| | | DESK. | MOSU01 | | / |
| | | ENVELOPE. | GAT | | / |
| | | LETTER OPENER, | ASG | | |
| 2 | | CHECKS. | ASA01 | 25 | / |
| | | CHECKS ALPHABETICALLY. | | | |
| | | ADD UP CHECKS ON CALCULATOR | CEAP01 | | / |
| | | CLEAR AND TOTAL. | CEAP03 | 3 | / |
| | | CHECKS ADD. | HSF | | |
| | | CHECKS. | GGM | 25 | / |
| | | ADDING MACHINE TAPE. | HTN | | / |
| | | TAPE OFF, AND | GAT | | / |
| 3 | | POST CHECKS IN JOURNAL | ODD | | / |
| | | DESK AND | GBT | | / |
| | | JOURNAL. | OBC01 | | / |
| | | JOURNAL, AND | LPBE | | |
| | | BLANK. | GMT | | / |
| | | PEN. | WSW01 | | 3 |
| | | CASH RECEIPTS FOR | WSD02 | | / |
| | | POSTED. | GBT | | |
| | | CHECKS, | PDN | | |
| | | ON CHECK, | | | |

RL  02/80

**Figure 9-11**

MCD-MOD II TASK CODING SHEET II

TASK NO [ ] [ ] [ ] [ ]  REV NO [ ] 19  TRANS TYPE [ ] 21

TASK NO: PCLE-II

| STEP | TITLE/DESCRIPTION/OBJECT | MCD CODE | Step Count | FREQUENCY |
|---|---|---|---|---|
| | POST CHECKS IN JOURNAL - CONTINUED | | | |
| 3 | OF FLEM AND | | | |
| | OF CHECK. | | | |
| | LINE UNDER AMOUNT, | PAN | | |
| | ADD AMOUNTS POSTED | PNA | | |
| 4 | CLEAR AND TOTAL. | WP | 25 | 1 |
| | ENTER AMOUNT. | CEAPO1 | | 1 |
| | TAPE, AND | CEAPO3 | | 1 |
| | OFF, | GGM | | 1 |
| 5 | WRAP UP | HTN | 25 | 1 |
| | PREVIOUS TAPE, | GST | | 1 |
| | TOTALS, AND | ERDS | | 6 |
| | EACH TOTAL. | EM | | 6 |
| | IF SAME. | EDS | | 1 |
| | TAPE IN WASTEBASKET. | GAT | | 1 |
| | TOTAL IN JOURNAL, | PNN | | 1 |
| | PEN AND TAPE. | GAT | | 1 |
| | DESK. | ODD | | 1 |
| | JOURNAL. | GIBT | | 1 |
| | CHECKS. | GBT | | 3 |
| | CHECKS TO ALIGN. | HJSO1 | | 1 |
| | TAPE TO CHECKS. | GSH | | 1 |
| | CHECKS. | FCP | | 1 |
| | CHECKS. | GAT | | 1 |

RL 02/80

PAGE 3 OF 3

Figure 9-12

phrases with the words that have been entered to create a task description and element description.

Once this is entered by Data Entry, the output (hard copy) will be Figures 9-13, 9-14, and 9-15. Naturally, any of this

GENERAL SALES CORPORATION                                    TASK NO. PCR—1
125 GENERAL BOULEVARD                                        POST CASH RECEIPTS
GENERAL CITY, ANYWHERE U.S.A.

DEPARTMENT. ACCOUNTING                          ANALYST. CLN
SECTION. PROCESSING                                    DATE CODED 10/8/99
JOB. POSTING CLERK                                EFFECTIVE DATE 12/1/99

ITEM COUNTED . CHECKS — ALL                        SUPERSEDES.
BATCH SIZE. 25   DAILY COUNT. 600                   SUPERSEDED BY.
HOW OFTEN DONE. ONCE PER CHECK

EQUIPMENT.   DESK, ELECTRONIC PRINTING CALCULATOR, OUT AND IN BASKET AND LETTER
             OPENER
MATERIAL.   CHECKS, JOURNAL, ENVELOPES, PEN AND RUBBER BANDS

STEP 1 — RECEIVE AND SORT CHECKS                                COUNT 25

| LN | DESCRIPTION | E | MCD CODE | FREQ. | U | TOTAL |
|----|-------------|---|----------|-------|---|-------|
| 1 | ENVELOPE. | | GST | 1 | | 36 |
| 2 | DESK. | | ODD | 1 | | 62 |
| 3 | ENVELOPE. | | MOSU01 | 1 | | 132 |
| 4 | LETTER OPENER. | | GAT | 1 | | 15 |
| 5 | CHECKS. | | ASG | 25 | | 1,175 |
| 6 | CHECKS. | | ASA01 | 25 | | 1,800 |
| | AVERAGE TIME PER ITEM 129 | | | TOTAL TIME | | 3,220 |

STEP 2 — ADD UP CHECKS ON CALCULATOR                            COUNT  25

| LN | DESCRIPTION | E | MCD CODE | FREQ. | U | TOTAL |
|----|-------------|---|----------|-------|---|-------|
| 1 | CHECKS. | | CEAP01 | 1 | | 21 |
| 2 | CHECKS. | | CEAP03 | 25 | | 725 |
| 3 | CHECKS. | | HSF | 25 | | 575 |
| 4 | ADDING MACHINE TAPE, | | GGM | 1 | | 18 |
| 5 | TAPE, AND | | HTN | 1 | | 23 |
| 6 | TAPE. | | GAT | 1 | | 15 |
| | AVERAGE TIME PER ITEM 55 | | | TOTAL TIME | | 1,377 |

STEP 3 — POST CHECKS IN  JOURNAL                                COUNT  25

| LN | DESCRIPTION | E | MCD CODE | FREQ. | U | TOTAL |
|----|-------------|---|----------|-------|---|-------|
| 1 | DESK AND | | ODD | 1 | | 62 |
| 2 | JOURNAL. | | GBT | 1 | | 46 |
| 3 | JOURNAL, AND | | OBC01 | 1 | | 48 |
| 4 | BLANK. | | LPBE | 1 | | 134 |
| 5 | PEN. | | GMT | 1 | | 33 |
| 6 | CASH RECEIPTS FOR, AND | | WSW01 | 3 | | 234 |
| 7 | POSTED. | | WSD02 | 1 | | 130 |
| 8 | CHECKS. | | GBT | 1 | | 46 |
| 9 | CHECK, | | PDN | 25 | | 3,600 |
| 10 | OF FIRM, AND | | PAN | 25 | | 8,975 |
| 11 | OF CHECK. | | PNA | 25 | | 3,225 |
| 12 | LINE UNDER AMOUNT. | | WP | 1 | | 15 |
| | AVERAGE TIME PER ITEM 662 | | | TOTAL TIME | | 16,548 |

MCD—MOD II TASK CODING SYSTEM                                      PAGE 1

Figure 9-13

output can be suppressed if desired. Also, if entered by a CRT on-line, you can display it on the CRT and then print it out if desired. On-line you can clean up any of the wording desired without affecting the program. As you see, the computer creates the task description using standard phrases

GENERAL SALES CORPORATION                                          TASK NO. PCR–1
125 GENERAL BOULEVARD                                              POST CASH RECEIPTS
GENERAL CITY, ANYWHERE U.S.A.

DEPARTMENT. ACCOUNTING                                ANALYST. CLN
SECTION. PROCESSING                                   DATE CODED 10/8/99
JOB. POSTING CLERK                                    EFFECTIVE DATE 12/1/99

ITEM COUNTED . CHECKS – ALL                           SUPERSEDES.
BATCH SIZE. 25  DAILY COUNT. 600                       SUPERSEDED BY.
HOW OFTEN DONE. ONCE PER CHECK

EQUIPMENT.   DESK, ELECTRONIC PRINTING CALCULATOR, OUT AND IN BASKET AND LETTER
             OPENER
MATERIAL.   CHECKS, JOURNAL, ENVELOPES, PEN AND RUBBER BANDS

STEP 4 – ADD AMOUNTS POSTED                                        COUNT   25

| LN | DESCRIPTION | E | MCD CODE | FREQ. | U | TOTAL |
|----|-------------|---|----------|-------|---|-------|
| 1 |  | | CEAP01 | 1 | | 21 |
| 2 | AMOUNT. | | CEAP03 | 25 | | 725 |
| 3 | TAPE, AND | | GGM | 1 | | 18 |
| 4 | OFF. | | HTN | 1 | | 23 |
| | AVERAGE TIME PER ITEM 31 | | | TOTAL TIME | | 787 |

STEP 5 – WRAP UP                                                  COUNT   25

| LN | DESCRIPTION | E | MCD CODE | FREQ. | U | TOTAL |
|----|-------------|---|----------|-------|---|-------|
| 1 | PREVIOUS TAPE. | | GST | 1 | | 36 |
| 2 | TOTALS AND | | ERDS | 6 | | 42 |
| 3 | EACH TOTAL. | | EM | 6 | | 6 |
| 4 | IF SAME. | | EDS | 1 | | 11 |
| 5 | TAPE IN WASTE BASKET. | | GAT | 1 | | 15 |
| 6 | TOTAL IN JOURNAL. | | PNN | 1 | | 193 |
| 7 | PEN AND TAPE. | | GAT | 1 | | 15 |
| 8 | DESK. | | ODD | 1 | | 62 |
| 9 | JOURNAL. | | GBT | 1 | | 46 |
| 10 | CHECKS. | | GBT | 1 | | 46 |
| 11 | CHECKS TO ALIGN | | HJS01 | 3 | | 24 |
| 12 | TAPE TO CHECKS. | | GSH | 1 | | 41 |
| 13 | CHECKS | | FRP | 1 | | 129 |
| 14 | CHECKS. | | GAT | 1 | | 15 |
| | AVERAGE TIME PER ITEM 27 | | | TOTAL TIME | | 681 |

| | |
|---|---|
| TASK TIME PER ITEM | 905 |
| ALLOWANCE (15%) | 136 |
| ALLOWED TIME | 1041 |
| STANDARD TIME | .01041 |
| ITEMS PER HOUR | 96.06 |

Figure 9-14

stored within the MCD-MOD-I data bank. If desired, you can write a narrative for each step.

The advantage of the computer is that it reduces the detail work of the analyst and keeps each standard in file for maintenance purposes or use in creating another similar standard.

GENERAL SALES CORPORATION                                    TASK NO. PCR–1
125 GENERAL BOULEVARD                                        POST CASH RECEIPTS
GENERAL CITY, ANYWHERE U.S.A.

DEPARTMENT. ACCOUNTING                        ANALYST.  CLN
SECTION.  PROCESSING                                    DATE CODED 10/8/99
JOB.  POSTING CLERK                                EFFECTIVE DATE 12/1/99

ITEM COUNTED . CHECKS  —  ALL                      SUPERSEDES.
BATCH SIZE.  25   DAILY COUNT.  600                SUPERSEDED BY.
HOW OFTEN DONE.  ONCE PER CHECK

EQUIPMENT.    DESK, ELECTRONIC PRINTING CALCULATOR, OUT AND IN BASKET AND LETTER
              OPENER
MATERIAL.   CHECKS, JOURNAL, ENVELOPES, PEN AND RUBBER BANDS

### TASK DESCRIPTION

STEP 1  —  RECEIVE AND SORT CHECKS

GET AND ASIDE ENVELOPE. OPEN AND CLOSE DESK DRAWER. OPEN ENVELOPE. ASIDE LETTER
OPENER. SORT CHECKS INTO GROUPS. PUT CHECKS IN ORDER.

STEP 2  —  ADD UP CHECKS ON CALCULATOR

CALCULATE CHECKS. CLEAR AND TOTAL. CALCULATE CHECKS ADD OR SUBTRACT. TURN
CHECKS. GET ADDING MACHINE TAPE, TEAR TAPE OFF, AND ASIDE TAPE.

STEP 3  —  POST CHECKS IN JOURNAL

OPEN AND CLOSE DESK DRAWER AND GET AND ASIDE JOURNAL. OPEN AND CLOSE JOURNAL
AND LOCATE PAGE BLANK. GET AND ASIDE PEN. WRITE CASH RECEIPTS FOR, WRITE NUMERIC DATE
POSTED. POST NUMERIC DATE ON CHECK, POST NAME OF FIRM, AND POST AMOUNT OF CHECK.
PUNCTUATE LINE UNDER AMOUNT.

STEP 4  —  ADD AMOUNTS POSTED

CALCULATE CLEAR AND TOTAL. CALCULATE ENTER AMOUNT. GET TAPE AND TEAR OFF.

STEP 5  —  WRAP UP

GET AND ASIDE PREVIOUS TAPE. READ TOTALS SILENTLY, MOVE EYES TO EACH TOTAL .
DECIDE IF SAME. ASIDE TAPE IN WASTE BASKET. POST TOTAL IN JOURNAL, ASIDE PEN AND TAPE.
OPEN AND CLOSE DESK DRAWER. GET AND ASIDE JOURNAL. G ET AND ASIDE CHECKS. JOB CHECKS
TO ALIGN. GET AND ASIDE TAPE TO CHECKS. BIND CHECKS WITH RUBBER BAND. ASIDE CHECKS.

                                        STANDARD TIME       .01041
                                        ITEMS PER HOUR       96.06

MCD–MOD II TASK CODING SYSTEM                                    PAGE 1

Figure 9-15

## chapter ten

# *What Is MCD-MOD-I?*

WE HAVE DISCUSSED how to measure an office task by using MCD-MOD-I manually or by use of the computer software known as MCD-MOD-II. In doing so we probably confused many of you, as no explanation of the MCD-MOD-I elements has been made. It would be very difficult to thoroughly familiarize you with all of the information relating to each element, but we can at least furnish you with their major purposes.

First, MCD-MOD-I is a catalog of standard work elements needed to measure the normal tasks found in an office. The elements are structured so they are universal in nature and can be combined to cover the specific methods required to perform office tasks.

All MCD-MOD-I elements are coded using the principles of alpha-mnemonic coding that was introduced by the author and R. M. Crossan [1] in the middle 1950s. Actually this coding takes advantage of the first letter of key words in the element description as a means of coding the element. Variations of the element are normally indicated by numbers following the code letters. Due to the use of numbers for variables, the coding system has also become known as alphanumeric.

In essence, the letters serve as a memory jogger for locating the work elements needed. In the case of MCD-MOD-I, the first letter of each code is basically an activity performed in an office environment. These first code letters and activities are:

| Code Letter | Activity |
|---|---|
| A | Arrange Papers |
| B | Body Elements |
| C | Calculate |
| D | Duplicate |
| E | Eye Times |
| F | Fasten/Unfasten |
| G | Get and Aside |
| H | Handle Paper |
| I | Insert |
| K | Keystrokes |
| L | Locate |
| M | Mailing |
| O | Open and Close |
| P | Post |
| R | Read |
| T | Type |
| W | Write |

[1]Richard M. Crossan and Harold W. Nance, *Master Standard Data*, (McGraw-Hill Book Company, Inc., 1962). Richard M. Crossan and Harold W. Nance, *Master Standard Data*, (McGraw-Hill Book Company, Inc., Revised, 1972). Richard M. Crossan and Harold W. Nance, *Master Standard Data*, (Robert E. Krieger Publishing Co., Inc., P.O. Box 9542, Melbourne, FL 32950, Reprinted, 1980).

So if you want to find an element for staple two papers together, you would need to think of the purpose of the staple. Obviously, it is to fasten the papers. So, stapling would be found under Fasten in MCD-MOD-I. By the same token, if you wish to remove a staple, this would be found under Fasten, as the opposite of Fasten is Unfasten. Using this logic, you will be able to follow the MCD-MOD-I data in Appendix A.

A brief description will now be given of each of the MCD-MOD-I activities covered.

## A—Arrange Papers

In office activities papers often have to be collated or sorted. The elements for measuring this can be found under Arrange Papers. Many of the elements cover several methods of collating and sorting. For our purpose it will suffice that for most collating and sorting found in an office, Arrange Papers will adequately measure the time required.

## B—Body Elements

Body Elements contains the elements needed to move the body from one location to another in an office environment. These elements cover movement of the body in an upright or seated position.

## C—Calculate

Calculate provides the elements needed to measure the use of electronic calculators of either the printing or nonprinting type. It also contains the elements for making simple mental calculations.

## D—Duplicate

With the wide variety of photocopying and printing equipment available today, Duplicate merely illustrates how this equipment is measured. Providing the work elements needed to cover all equipment would be a monumental undertaking.

## E—Eye Times

The use of the eyes in the office is a very important part of performing the majority of the tasks. These Eye Times will cover over 95 percent of the conditions found for reading and comparing information.

## F—Fasten/Unfasten

This category of elements covers the majority of the devices used in the office to fasten papers together. The category also covers the removal (unfastening) of these devices.

## G—Get and Aside

These elements provide the time for releasing previous object, moving the hand to the next object, and gaining control of the next object—Get. Elements are also included for moving the object to a location—Aside. To simplify this category, the two are also combined.

## H—Handle Paper

These elements can also, except for five elements, be referred to as massage paper elements. Elements for jogging, folding, tearing, and shifting paper or the hands on paper are all provided for. In addition, the cutting, drilling, and punching of paper are included.

## I—Insert

These elements cover the inserting and removing of papers from files, binders, or machines. They are normally used in conjunction with Locate. The elements cover individual papers, groups of papers, or folders.

## K—Keystrokes

Keystrokes provides for operating of individual keys on calculators, typewriters, word processors, keypunch, CRTs, or any key-operated device. With the vast changes occurring in key-operated equipment, it is necessary to be equipped to analyze each properly.

## L—Locate

Locate contains elements for locating cards or folders in files, pages in books or loose in folders, and elements that are often performed during the locating of information. As previously mentioned, this category often occurs with Insert.

## M—Mailing

The elements within Mailing deal with things that are done to prepare mail, open mail, or identify mail. These cover normal activities related to mail of either the internal or external variety.

## O—Open and Close

The elements within this category deal with items that are opened in the office. All times are for both opening and closing, as after use most are closed.

# P—Post

This is a combination of eye and write times involved in reading information and writing it down on another document. These are common elements found in accounting, customer service, or activities related to information preparation.

# R—Read

These elements are combinations of basic eye times to read the various items normally read in an office. The times do not include comparisons or decisions related to what is read.

# T—Type

The elements found in this data are those needed for measuring of various kinds of typing. These elements can easily be combined into typing standard data tailored to meet a particular firm's needs.

# W—Write

These elements cover the various kinds of information written as well as basic writing or printing of letters. Write combined with Read, however, will not result in the same times as shown on Post, as the time for movement of eyes between documents will be missing.

## Time Units Used

MCD-MOD-I has been developed by combining basic MTM motions into standard elements tailored to office conditions. Therefore, the time untis are those of MTM known as Time Measurement Units (TMU for short). They can be converted

to seconds, minutes, or hours by multiplying the TMU values
by the following:

| Time Unit | Multiplying Factor |
|-----------|--------------------|
| Seconds | .036 |
| Minutes | .0006 |
| Hours | .00001 |

In other words, 100,000 TMU would be 3,600 seconds
(100,000 × .036), 60 minutes (100,000 × .0006) or 1 hour
(100,000 × .00001).

## chapter eleven

# Kinds of Reports for Using the Task Standards

WE HAVE DISCUSSED how information concerning the tasks performed in an office is gathered and how this is used to measure the time required to perform the tasks. We briefly discussed feedback (reporting) and controls in Chapter 2; however, we need to investigate this thoroughly.

What we must decide in our productivity improvement program is the ultimate use we wish to make of the resulting task standards. This will determine the kind of feedback (reporting) and controls we will ultimately need.

For example, if our goal is merely to maintain proper staffing of all areas so as to utilize our employees properly, then our feedback (reporting) and controls have only to indicate the progress of each department in meeting our goals. This means that we need only weekly or monthly performance reports for each department.

On the other hand, if we wish to utilize the standards to provide an opportunity for supervisors to assist employees in improving and a means for employees to know how they are progressing, we need more elaborate feedback (reporting) and controls.

If we wish to utilize the results to compensate good performers, control costs and quality, etc., then our feedback (reporting) and controls become even more elaborate.

The use of measurement results will depend upon the end results desired by your firm. These end results may and should change through the passage of time. Therefore, we will present the various feedback (reporting) and controls that are in common use. These, naturally, should be tailored to your firm's true needs.

The various feedback (reporting) and controls will be discussed as:

- Reporting and Controls on an Individual Basis;
- Reporting and Controls on an Area Basis; and
- Reporting and Controls on a Departmental Basis.

In order to do this in a meaningful manner, we will use the following as our fictional company breakdown:

| Department | Sections | No. of Employees |
|---|---|---|
| Corporate Services | Document Processing | 16 |
| | Mail Room | 15 |
| | Reproduction | 10 |
| | Supply Room | 5 |
| Operations | New Account Entry | 20 |
| | Preparation of New Account | 70 |
| | Issuing of New Account | 20 |
| | Purchasing | 10 |
| Finance | Account Billing | 10 |
| | Accounts Receivable | 6 |

|  | Accounts Payable | 6 |
|---|---|---|
|  | Financial Reports | 7 |
| Sales | Customer Service | 5 |
|  | Sales Correspondence | 10 |
|  | Advertising Preparation | 10 |

These are the areas within our firm that would be covered by measurement. As you see, this is a total of 220 employees. For our illustrations we will use a 40-hour week as normal for each employee.

## Reporting and Controls on an Individual Basis

For sound reporting and controls on an individual basis, we need to know how each individual spends his or her time during each working day. We also need to know what each person worked on and how much of each item was produced (completed). With standards for most tasks, the time we really need to know about is that spent on work not related to tasks having standards. In most offices the time spent on work not covered by standards is recorded on a sign out sheet.

Figure 11-1 is a typical sign out sheet. This sheet is normally kept on the supervisor's desk so supervision will have some control over the correct reporting of time spent doing the work not covered by standards. We have recorded on Figure 11-1 times spent by members of our fictional document processing section of the Corporate Services Department. Later on we will tie in these entries with the complete reporting of individuals.

Figure 11-2 is a Daily Production Record which each employee fills out each day. On Figure 11-2 we have selected the Document Processing Section to tie in with Figure 11-1. You will note that each measured task is shown, and the employee records the total of each task he or she did during a day.

The Daily Sign Out Sheet (Figure 11-1) and Daily Production Record (Figure 11-2) are normally summarized by the

4-14-77
DATE

DAILY SIGN OUT SHEET

| EMPLOYEE | TIME OFF | TIME ON | ELAPSED TIME | REASON FOR OFF STANDARDS | SUPERVISOR APPROVAL |
|---|---|---|---|---|---|
|  | 8 00 | 8 18 | .3 | Late | S D |
| Paula Iris | 10 06 | 10 30 | .4 | No Work | S D |
|  | 3 15 |  | .8 | No Work | S D |
|  | 4 30 |  |  |  |  |
|  |  | 8 00 |  |  |  |
| Joyce Adams | 10 12 | 11 24 | 1.2 | Discussion with Supr. | S D |
|  | 2 30 | 3 00 | .5 | No Work | S D |
|  | 4 30 |  |  |  |  |
|  |  |  |  |  |  |
| Kathy Hunt | absent | | 7.5 | Sickness | S D |
|  |  |  |  |  |  |
|  |  |  |  |  |  |
|  |  | 8 00 |  |  |  |
| Alice Jones | 8 30 | 9 00 | .5 | Machine Trouble | S D |
|  | 4 30 |  |  |  |  |
|  |  |  |  |  |  |
|  |  | 8 00 |  |  |  |
| Edna Brown | 9 10 | 9 40 | .5 | Special "XYZ" Report | S D |
| O.T. 4 30 - 7 00 | 11 10 | 11 45 | .7 | " " " | S D |
| 2½ Hrs. | 7 00 |  |  |  |  |
|  |  | 8 00 |  |  |  |
| Ann Frank | 4 30 |  |  |  |  |
|  |  |  |  |  |  |
|  |  |  |  |  |  |
|  |  | 8 00 |  |  |  |
| Terry Oster | 4 30 |  |  |  |  |
|  |  |  |  |  |  |
|  |  |  |  |  |  |
|  |  | 8 00 |  |  |  |
| Eileen Love | 2 00 |  | 2.0 | Dentist Appointment | S D |
|  | 4 30 |  |  |  |  |
|  |  |  |  |  |  |

Fig. 11-1                     Display 6 — 4
SABCO / Management Consultants

Figure 11-1

supervisor. These sheets are then turned over to the productivity improvement group on either a daily or weekly basis.

The productivity improvement group reviews the Daily
Production Record and Daily Sign Out Sheets for any ab-
normal production counts or excessive off-standard times.
These, if they occur, are then reviewed with the supervisor

# DAILY PRODUCTION RECORD

**EMPLOYEE** Joyce Adams

**DEPARTMENT OR SECTION** Corporate Services – Document Processing

**DATE** 4-14-99

| TASK NO | NAME OF TASK | ITEMS COUNTED | NUMBER OF ITEMS PROCESSED | | | | | TOTALS |
|---|---|---|---|---|---|---|---|---|
| 1 | Post Cash Receipts | Checks | (25) - 32 - 23 - 40 - 22 | | | | | 142 |
| 2 | Process Applications | Apps | | | | | | |
| 3 | Type Advices | Notices | ++++ ++++ // | | | | | 12 |
| 4 | Log In Documents | Documents | 6 - 3 - 8 - 1 | | | | | 18 |
| 5 | Process Small Orders | Orders | | | | | | |
| 6 | Process "A" Documents | Documents | | | | | | |
| 7 | Process "B" Documents | Documents | 130 - (126) | | | | | 256 |
| 8 | Handle Rejects | Notices | | | | | | |
| 9 | Trip to Keypunch | Trips | / | | | | | 1 |
| 10 | File Completed Documents | Documents | | | | | | |
| | | | | | | | | |
| | | | | | | | | |
| | | | | | | | | |
| | | | | | | | | |
| | | | | | | | | |
| | | | | | | | | |
| | | | | | | | | |
| | | | | | | | | |

**Approved By** Sue Downes  Supervisor

4-15-99  Date

**Figure 11-2**

and any required corrections are made. On counts this can normally be checked by random audit of work received and completed. After all documents are reviewed, then they are either recapped manually or turned over to Data Processing for developing the individual reports. We will go through the manual version so you can appreciate what is involved.

Each of the daily production records is recorded on a Weekly Production and Time Record (Figure 11-3). In fact, the totals on Figure 11-2 appear under "Wed." on Figure 11-3 on the left side. All of these are then totaled across for each task, and the total multiplied by the "Time Std." to obtain the "Std. Hours." The Daily Sign Out Sheets (Figure 11-1) are then used to complete the time section on the right of Figure 11-3. Figure 11-1 provided the entry for "Wed."

Finally, all the weekly production and time records for each employee in the Document Processing Section are entered on the Weekly Performance Report (Figure 11-4). As you will note, Figure 11-3 supplied the information for Joyce Adams.

As you can see, only three people in Document Processing have performances within what we discussed previously as being in the acceptable range. It is also interesting to note that the supervisor, Sue Downes, performed work that was on standard at a level of 68 percent performance. Obviously this work should have been assigned others, as Sue Downes should spend her time supervising. A good area for this supervision would be finding out why there are so many low performers and assisting them to improve.

## Reporting and Controls on an Area Basis

Reporting on an area basis would mean that our report for Document Processing would indicate only the totals shown on Figure 11-4. To obtain these totals we would need a report from Document Processing similar to Figure 11-5, Section

# WEEKLY PRODUCTION AND TIME RECORD

DEPARTMENT: CORPORATE SERVICES  
SECTION: DOCUMENT PROCESSING  
EMPLOYEE: Joyce Adams  
WEEK STARTING MONDAY: 4-12-99

| TASK | NO. | MON. | TUES. | WED. | THUR. | FRI. | SAT. | SUN. | (A) TOTAL ITEMS | (B) TIME STD. | (A×B) STD. HOURS |
|------|-----|------|-------|------|-------|------|------|------|------|------|------|
| PCR | 1 | 191 | 197 | 142 | 93 | 86 | | | 509 | .010 | (5.1) |
| PA | 2 | | | | | | | | 115 | .100 | |
| TA | 3 | 10 | 16 | 12 | 14 | 12 | | | 52 | .100 | (5.2) |
| LID | 4 | 18 | 17 | 18 | 12 | 12 | | | 77 | .156 | (12.0) |
| PSO | 5 | | | | | | | | 017 | .017 | |
| PAD | 6 | | | | | | | | 003 | .003 | |
| PBD | 7 | 190 | 220 | 256 | 212 | 75 | | | 893 | .012 | (10.7) |
| HR | 8 | | | | | | | | 386 | .386 | |
| TK | 9 | 1 | 1 | 1 | 3 | 1 | | | 7 | .300 | (2.1) |
| FCD | 10 | | | | | | | | 012 | .012 | |
| | | | | | | | | | | | |
| | | | | | | | | | | | |
| | | | | | | | | | | | |
| | | | | | | | | | | | |
| | | | | | | | | | (A × B) TOTAL STANDARD HOURS | | (35.1) |

APPROVED BY: JD JD JD JD JD  
DATE APPROVED: 4/12 4/13 4/14 4/15 4/16

| | MON. | TUE. | WED. | THUR. | FRI. | SAT. | SUN. | TOTAL |
|---|------|------|------|-------|------|------|------|-------|
| (C) TOTAL SCHED. HRS | 8.0 | 8.0 | 8.0 | 8.0 | 8.0 | | | 40.0 |
| (D) ABSENT/ LOANED HRS | | | | | | | | |
| (E) SUPER- VISORY HRS | | | | | | | | |
| (F) UNMEAS. HRS NO. STND | .3 | | | | .2 | | | .5 |
| (G) UNMEAS. HRS OTHER | | .3 | 1.7 | | | | | 2.0 |
| | | | | | | | | 37.5 |

ACTUAL HOURS = C–(D+E+F+G)

REMARKS

SUPERVISOR'S INITIALS & DATE: JD 4-19-99

$$\text{(H) ACTUAL HOURS} \quad 37.5$$

$$\frac{\text{(H+F+G) ACTUAL HOURS + UNMEASURED HOURS} \quad 40.0}{\text{(H) ACTUAL HOURS} \quad 37.5} = \text{COVERAGE} \quad 94\%$$

$$\frac{\text{(A×B) STANDARD HOURS} \quad 35.1}{\text{(H) ACTUAL HOURS} \quad 37.5} = \text{PERFORMANCE} \quad 94\%$$

Figure 11-3

Display 6 – 6

105

WEEKLY PERFORMANCE REPORT – A

| EMPLOYEE | TOTAL (C) | ABSENT/ LOANED (D) | SUPERVISORY (E) | UNMEASURED (F) | (G) | ACTUAL (H) | STANDARD (AXB) | % COVERAGE H÷(F+G+H) | % PERFORMANCE (AXB)÷H |
|---|---|---|---|---|---|---|---|---|---|
| Joyce Adams | 40.0 | | | .5 | 2.0 | 37.5 | 35.1 | 94 | 94 |
| Edna Brown | 48.0 | | | | 2.8 | 45.2 | 34.8 | 94 | 77 |
| Mary Carr | 44.0 | | | | .7 | 43.3 | 31.0 | 98 | 71 |
| Sue Downes | 44.0 | | 33.0 | | | 11.0 | 7.5 | 100 | 68 |
| Grace Eden | 42.0 | 15.0 | | | | 27.0 | 16.2 | 100 | 60 |
| Ann Frank | 44.0 | | | | | 44.0 | 21.2 | 100 | 48 |
| Rose Green | 44.0 | | | | | 44.0 | 18.5 | 100 | 42 |
| Kathy Hunt | 46.0 | 7.5 | 22.0 | | | 16.5 | 6.9 | 100 | 42 |
| Paula Iris | 40.0 | 7.5 | | 2.2 | 3.5 | 26.8 | 11.0 | 80 | 41 |
| Alice Jones | 40.0 | | | | 2.0 | 38.0 | 15.2 | 95 | 40 |
| Jackie Kerin | 40.0 | | | 8.5 | | 31.5 | 12.6 | 77 | 40 |
| Eileen Love | 40.0 | 10.0 | | 8.3 | | 21.7 | 8.5 | 72 | 39 |
| Pam Mason | 40.0 | | | .5 | | 39.5 | 15.1 | 99 | 38 |
| Nora North | 40.0 | | | | 3.7 | 36.3 | 13.8 | 91 | 38 |
| Terry Oster | 40.0 | | | | | 40.0 | 15.2 | 100 | 38 |
| Karen Pope | 40.0 | | | | | 40.0 | 13.2 | 100 | 33 |
| (16) TOTALS | 672.0 | 40.0 | 55.0 | 22.3 | 12.4 | 542.3 | 275.8 | 94 | 51 |

DEPARTMENT: CORPORATE SERVICES
SECTION: DOCUMENT PROCESSING
SUPERVISOR: SUE DOWNES
WEEK STARTING MONDAY 4-12-99

COMMENTS

Performance Last Week – (First Week)

Display 7 – 1

Figure 11-4

---

SECTION WEEKLY PRODUCTION AND TIME RECORD

| TASK | NO. | MON. | TUE. | WED. | THU. | FRI. | SAT. | SUN. | (A) Total Items | (B) Time Std. | (A x B) Std. Hours |
|---|---|---|---|---|---|---|---|---|---|---|---|
| PCR | 1 | 450 | 420 | 444 | 470 | 406 | | | 2,190 | .010 | 21.90 |
| PA | 2 | 48 | 51 | 49 | 52 | 50 | | | 250 | .115 | 28.75 |
| TA | 3 | 196 | 212 | 190 | 226 | 196 | | | 1,020 | .100 | 102.00 |
| LID | 4 | 20 | 17 | 25 | 15 | 18 | | | 95 | .156 | 14.82 |
| PSO | 5 | 200 | 160 | 190 | 170 | 180 | | | 900 | .017 | 15.30 |
| PAD | 6 | 130 | 170 | 150 | 160 | 140 | | | 750 | .003 | 2.25 |
| PBD | 7 | 390 | 404 | 380 | 410 | 401 | | | 1,985 | .012 | 23.82 |
| HR | 8 | 25 | 28 | 30 | 29 | 26 | | | 138 | .386 | 53.27 |
| TK | 9 | 6 | 8 | 14 | 6 | 8 | | | 42 | .300 | 12.60 |
| FCD | 10 | 19 | 20 | 15 | 16 | 21 | | | 91 | .012 | 1.09 |

DEPARTMENT: Corporate Services
SECTION: Document Processing
TOTAL EMPLOYEES: 16
WEEK STARTING MONDAY: 4/12/99

| | MON. | TUE. | WED. | THU. | FRI. | SAT. | SUN. | TOTAL |
|---|---|---|---|---|---|---|---|---|
| (C) Total Sched. Hours | 136 | 132 | 132 | 138 | 134 | – | – | 672.0 |
| (D) Absent/ Loaned Hrs. | 10.0 | 8.0 | 6.0 | 10.0 | 6.0 | – | – | 40.0 |
| (E) Supervisory Hours | 12 | 13 | 10 | 10 | 10 | – | – | 55.0 |
| (F) Unmeasured Hrs. No Std. | 4.5 | 4.3 | 4.6 | 4.0 | 4.9 | – | – | 22.3 |
| (G) Unmeasured Hrs. Other | 2.4 | 2.8 | 2.6 | 2.5 | 2.1 | – | – | 12.4 |
| (H) Actual Hours = C – (D+E+F+G) | | | | | | | | 542.3 |

REMARKS

SUPERVISORS' INITIALS & DATE: SD  4/19/99

| (H) Actual Hours | | (H+F+G) Actual Hours + Unmeasured Hours | | Coverage |
|---|---|---|---|---|
| 542.3 | ÷ | 577.0 | = | 94% |

| (A x B) Standard Hours | | (H) Actual Hours | | Performance |
|---|---|---|---|---|
| 275.8 | ÷ | 542.3 | = | 51% |

APPROVED BY: SD SD SD SD SD
DATE APPROVED: 4/12  4/13  4/14  4/15  4/16

(A x B) Total Standard Hours: 275.80

Figure 11-5

WEEKLY PERFORMANCE SUMMARY REPORT

| DEPARTMENT | | | | SECTION | | | | CCC | SUPERVISOR | |
|---|---|---|---|---|---|---|---|---|---|---|
| Corporate Services | | | | Document Processing | | | | | Sue Downes | |
| WEEK ENDING | TOTAL EMPLOYEES ASSIGNED | HOURS | | | | | | | % COVERAGE | % PERFORMANCE |
| | | TOTAL | ABSENT/ LOANED | SUPERVISORY | UNMEASURED | | ACTUAL | STANDARD | | |
| | | | | | NO STANDARD | OTHER | | | | |
| 4-18-99 | 16 | 672.0 | 40.0 | 55.0 | 22.3 | 12.4 | 542.3 | 276.3 | 94 | 51 |
| 4-25-99 | 16 | 660.0 | 41.5 | 52.0 | 22.0 | 2.8 | 541.7 | 281.4 | 96 | 52 |
| 5-2-99 | 16 | 652.0 | 42.0 | 55.0 | 25.6 | 5.0 | 526.4 | 280.3 | 95 | 53 |
| 5-9-99 | 15 | 635.0 | 42.0 | 57.5 | 6.8 | 2.0 | 516.7 | 276.9 | 98 | 54 |
| 5-16-99 | 15 | 610.0 | 31.0 | 51.0 | 4.0 | .5 | 523.5 | 284.1 | 99 | 54 |
| 5-23-99 | 15 | 600.0 | 82.5 | 53.0 | 4.3 | 3.4 | 456.8 | 277.5 | 98 | 61 |
| 5-30-99 | 14 | 582.0 | 65.8 | 52.0 | 6.2 | 4.2 | 453.8 | 281.8 | 98 | 62 |
| 6-6-99 | 14 | 560.0 | 60.0 | 53.5 | 6.0 | 2.0 | 438.5 | 280.3 | 98 | 64 |
| 6-13-99 | 13 | 530.0 | 40.0 | 50.0 | 8.1 | 20.4 | 411.5 | 282.6 | 94 | 69 |
| 6-20-99 | 13 | 530.0 | 66.5 | 51.5 | 7.8 | 37.2 | 367.0 | 279.4 | 89 | 76 |
| 6-27-99 | 13 | 520.0 | 44.0 | 50.0 | 9.3 | 27.8 | 389.0 | 281.0 | 91 | 72 |
| 7-4-99 | 13 | 484.0 | 40.0 | 54.0 | 7.6 | 39.0 | 332.4 | 280.0 | 85 | 84 |
| 7-11-99 | 12 | 480.0 | 32.0 | 51.5 | 11.3 | 52.6 | 332.1 | 283.5 | 84 | 85 |

| COMMENTS | | | | | | | | | | |
|---|---|---|---|---|---|---|---|---|---|---|
| | | | | | | | | | | |

| ISSUED BY | DATE | |
|---|---|---|
| G. Campbell, Mgr., Work Measurement | 7-13-99 | |

Display 7 – 2

**Figure 11-6**

Weekly Production and Time Record. The source for this would be the supervisor.

The calculations shown on Figure 11-5 would be made by the productivity group. The results would then appear on a Weekly Performance Summary Report similar to Figure 11-6. Our calculations on Figure 11-5 appear as the first line on this report.

This would not provide the supervisor with who the low performers are, but it would serve as a basis for improving. This would furnish all the information needed by the department head. In fact, this is the kind of reporting needed by department heads.

On an area (section) basis, often the reporting can be simplified if desired. For example, if the week beginning 4/12/99 is a typical average week for document processing, then we could use the count of only Post Cash Receipts of checks and establish one standard for Document Processing. This standard would be .126 hour (275.8 ÷ 2,190). using this, you would need only to count the number of checks posted per week, but periodically all items should be counted for several weeks and the average standard updated.

## Reporting and Controls on a Departmental Basis

The departmental report is normally prepared from combining the area (section reports similar to Figure 11-6 for Document Processing) and all other sections into a consolidated report. Figure 11-7 is an example of a report where all sections of corporate services are combined. This report would be used by the head of corporate services to improve and control the areas through his or her section heads and supervisors.

This report would be of little value to determine how each section is doing or for the section supervisors to take action. It would be worthwhile to determine whether or not corporate services is overstaffed. To determine this you would need to

CONSOLIDATED WEEKLY PERFORMANCE REPORT

| DEPARTMENT: Corporate Services | | SECTIONS: Mail Room, Supply Room, Reproduction, Document Processing | | | | | CCC | | DEPARTMENT HEAD: John Jones | |
|---|---|---|---|---|---|---|---|---|---|---|
| WEEK ENDING | TOTAL EMPLOYEES ASSIGNED | HOURS | | | | | | | % COVERAGE | % PERFORMANCE |
| | | TOTAL | ABSENT/ LOANED | SUPERVISORY | UNMEASURED | | ACTUAL | STANDARD | | |
| | | | | | NO STANDARD | OTHER | | | | |
| 4-18-99 | 46 | 1,932.0 | 115.0 | 150.0 | 69.3 | 28.5 | 1,569.2 | 800.3 | 94 | 51 |
| 4-25-99 | 46 | 1,875.0 | 105.0 | 148.0 | 55.3 | 16.9 | 1,549.8 | 805.9 | 96 | 52 |
| 5-2-99 | 46 | 1,870.0 | 110.0 | 150.0 | 69.8 | 20.6 | 1,519.6 | 805.4 | 94 | 53 |
| 5-9-99 | 43 | 1,750.0 | 110.0 | 155.0 | 27.8 | 10.5 | 1,446.7 | 781.2 | 97 | 54 |
| 5-16-99 | 43 | 1,730.0 | 105.0 | 145.0 | 25.6 | 5.5 | 1,448.9 | 782.4 | 98 | 54 |
| 5-23-99 | 43 | 1,720.0 | 230.0 | 149.0 | 26.3 | 10.2 | 1,304.5 | 795.7 | 97 | 61 |
| 5-30-99 | 40 | 1,680.0 | 195.0 | 148.0 | 28.6 | 12.6 | 1,295.8 | 803.4 | 97 | 62 |
| 6-6-99 | 40 | 1,600.0 | 185.0 | 150.0 | 27.9 | 10.5 | 1,226.6 | 790.0 | 97 | 64 |
| 6-13-99 | 37 | 1,517.0 | 125.0 | 142.0 | 32.1 | 36.8 | 1,181.1 | 815.6 | 94 | 69 |
| 6-20-99 | 37 | 1,517.0 | 196.0 | 148.0 | 30.6 | 49.2 | 1,093.2 | 831.0 | 93 | 76 |
| 6-27-99 | 37 | 1,480.0 | 115.0 | 142.0 | 39.6 | 47.2 | 1,136.2 | 818.0 | 93 | 72 |
| 7-4-99 | 35 | 1,400.0 | 100.0 | 145.0 | 38.4 | 92.5 | 1,024.1 | 870.0 | 89 | 85 |
| 7-11-99 | 35 | 1,400.0 | 100.0 | 140.0 | 45.6 | 106.2 | 1,008.2 | 877.1 | 87 | 87 |

COMMENTS:

ISSUED BY: C. Campbell, Mgr., Work Measurement    DATE: 7-13-99

Figure 11-7

know what the staff should be, and this would best be determined from a Consolidated Staffing Report. This could be developed using Figure 11-7 as the basis. To do this we would need to establish our company goals for coverage, performance level, supervisory time, and absentee time. We will use the following to illustrate a consolidated staffing report:

| Item | Goal |
|------|------|
| Coverage | 85 percent |
| Performance | 85 percent |
| Supervision | 40 hours/section |
| Absenteeism | 40 hours/week |

Using this as a basis, our formula for standard staff (what the staff should be) is:

$$\text{Standard Staff} = (\frac{\text{Total Standard Hours}}{.85 \times .85} + \text{No. of sections} \times$$

$$40 \text{ hours} + 40 \text{ hours}) \div 40 \text{ hours/week/employee}.$$

Using this formula and Figure 11-7 we can create the Consolidated Stafing Report, Figure 11-8.

In referring to Figure 11-8, obviously our work load (number of items handled) gradually increased as did our performance. Our coverage fell, but it is still above our expected 85 percent. The last two weeks also indicate that we do not have enough people on the staff. This is good, as our true goal should be 100 percent performance and 85 percent or above coverage. This being the case, then we do not need staff.

## Summary

In this chapter we have discussed several reports that may be generated for monitoring and controlling a productivity improvement program. These are not all of the reports that are

CONSOLIDATED STAFFING REPORT

| ORGANIZATION | | | DEPARTMENT Corporate Services | | SECTIONS Document Processing, Mail Room, Supply Room, Reproduction | | ADMINISTRATOR John Strong | | |
|---|---|---|---|---|---|---|---|---|---|
| WEEK ENDING | % PERFORMANCE | % COVERAGE | NUMBER OF EMPLOYEES | | | | ANNUAL TOTAL HOURS | | CUMULATIVE SAVINGS TO DATE |
| | | | PRESENT STAFF | STANDARD STAFF | REDUCED STAFF | EXCESS | POTENTIAL SAVINGS | ACTUAL SAVINGS | |
| 4-18-99 | 51 | 94 | 46 | 32.7 | 0 | 13.3 | 27,664 | --- | --- |
| 4-25-99 | 52 | 96 | 46 | 32.9 | 0 | 13.1 | 27,248 | --- | --- |
| 5-2-99 | 53 | 94 | 46 | 32.9 | 0 | 13.1 | 27,248 | --- | --- |
| 5-9-99 | 54 | 97 | 43 | 32.0 | 3 | 11.0 | 22,880 | 6,240 | 120 |
| 5-16-99 | 54 | 98 | 43 | 32.1 | 3 | 10.9 | 22,672 | 6,240 | 240 |
| 5-23-99 | 61 | 97 | 43 | 32.5 | 3 | 10.5 | 21,840 | 6,240 | 360 |
| 5-30-99 | 62 | 97 | 40 | 32.8 | 6 | 7.2 | 14,976 | 12,480 | 600 |
| 6-6-99 | 64 | 97 | 40 | 32.3 | 6 | 7.7 | 16,016 | 12,480 | 840 |
| 6-13-99 | 69 | 94 | 37 | 33.2 | 9 | 3.8 | 7,904 | 18,720 | 1,200 |
| 6-20-99 | 76 | 93 | 37 | 33.8 | 9 | 3.2 | 6,656 | 18,720 | 1,560 |
| 6-27-99 | 72 | 93 | 37 | 33.3 | 9 | 3.7 | 7,696 | 18,720 | 1,920 |
| 7-4-99 | 85 | 89 | 35 | 35.1 | 11 | - .1 | - 208 | 22,880 | 2,360 |
| 7-11-99 | 87 | 87 | 35 | 35.3 | 11 | - .3 | - 624 | 22,880 | 2,800 |

COMMENTS:

ISSUED BY: C. Campbell, Mgr., Work Measurement        DATE 7-13-99

Figure 11-8

possible, but they are the basic ones for having reports and controls at the levels discussed.

In the very early stages of a productivity improvement program it is recommended:

1. That reporting be on an individual employee basis until an area has consistently performed overall at an acceptable performance and coverage level—if incentives are involved on an individual basis, then individual reporting will become a way of life;

2. That section or department reporting be used for management above the first line supervisory level except where individual reporting is no longer necessary; and

3. That when major changes in systems and/or procedures take place in an area or when overall performance and/or coverage start to decline, the area reverts to individual reporting and controls until satisfactory conditions are again consistent within that area.

As a productivity improvement program progresses, your productivity improvement group should be constantly auditing progress and looking for methods of simplifying reporting and controls. In the example of Document Processing, this section reported their production count for 10 different tasks, and this is probably very necessary on individual reporting. However, if the section were switched to reporting as a group, then it is very possible that all you need count is how many checks are handled and relate other tasks to the checks.

A word of caution is in order. If you simplify by combining task standards, make sure this is audited to assure that relationships are correct. In fact, all standards should be audited at least once per year, as conditions in a progressive firm are never static.

## chapter twelve

# How the Reports Are Used To Improve Productivity

IT HAS BEEN PROVEN time and time again that individuals will improve their productivity if they are aware that their peers or superiors are observing how they are producing. If you have no form of reporting in your firm but know from past history that 200 items are handled per day, chances are this 200 will increase if you ask the employees to report how many are done each day. True, you will have certain individuals who have a fixed work pace, and they will never alter this pace. These individuals are in the minority, and let's hope the discrimination laws do not cover these individuals in relation to work.

In essence, improvements will be made just by installing reporting and controls based on measurement. These improvements will come faster, however, if supervision utilizes the reports correctly. Supervision should use the reports to discuss with each employee his or her overall progress and ascertain any difficulties the person may be having and provide assistance where possible in overcoming these difficulties. The satisfactory performers should naturally be congratulated, but they may wish to discuss difficulties they are having that prohibit them from doing even better.

The important thing in discussing progress with both the high and low performers is taking a positive attitude in the discussion. For example, when talking with a high performer, it is far better to say:

"Your performance is satisfactory, but are there any improvements that would aid you in doing even better?"

rather than:

"Your performance is excellent, keep up the good work."

In the first statement you imply that the employee is performing well but could possibly do even better. In the second statement you imply that the employee is at his or her peak. We all feel we can do better even if we cannot.

When approaching the low performer, again, you must be positive. It is far better to say:

"You are making progress, and we would like to assist you in overcoming any difficulties that will aid in further improving your progress."

rather than:

"Your performance is inadequate: what do you plan to do to improve it?"

The first statement, if made correctly, implies that you want to assist. The second is more or less a threat.

Just talking with each individual in the supervisor's office is not enough. The supervisor needs to spend time with each individual at his or her work place. This time will be spent giving specific assistance in overcoming any real difficulties the employee may be having. In other words, truly put forth an effort to assist the employees.

If no measurable improvement is made after a considerable effort to assist a low performer, then it may be desirable to review all conditions relating to that employee. Naturally, we assume all other employees are progressing in performance. First of all, we need to find out whether or not the employee is over or under qualified for the job. This can best be done by reviewing the employee's file with your Personnel Department. In reviewing the file and discussing it with Personnel, look carefully at the employee's education and past work history. The employee may have too much or too little education for the job assigned or may have a work history of poor performance at similar work in the past.

At this point you are probably saying, "Personnel looked at this when they employed this individual." True, they looked at the education level and past work history but only as they pertained to your overall employer criteria. It is very doubtful that Personnel considered this in light of a specific job. In reality, more often than not Personnel is finding people to fill employment requisitions rather than specific jobs. It is only in highly technical or professional openings that they look for specifics in individuals.

If either the education or past work history indicates that the employee is in the wrong job, then work out with Personnel a transfer to a more desirable position. The chances are the employee will be happier. By all means do not discharge the employee because he or she is not in the right job. This could result in an overall deterioration of both productivity and morale.

If the investigation of the employee's education and work history sheds no light on the subject, then it is time to have a serious talk with the employee. Again, the supervisor must be positive and not indicate any negative attitude. Start by saying,

"Your performance is remaining about the same week in and week out even though we are positive you can do better. Is there some problem you are having that you wish to discuss?"

If the employee says,

"No."

then the supervisor might say,

"I do not mean a problem at work but possibly a personal problem. Naturally, if you wish to discuss it, it will be strictly confidential."

If the employee starts to say something and then says,

"Well, yes, but I prefer not to discuss it."

then the supervisor should say,

"I respect your decision not to discuss it, but would appreciate your making a better effort to improve."

Chances are that eventually this employee will come to the supervisor and discuss the problem. At any rate, an honest effort has been made to truly assist the employee. This by no means covers all the ways the supervisor can approach and assist employees. It merely scratches the surface.

Basically, the first step in utilizing the reports and controls based on measurement is to improve the performance of individuals. As we discussed in an earlier chapter, offices without any form of measurement and controls normally have a performance in the 50 to 60 percent. Thus our initial efforts are to increase this performance level to an acceptable level of 70 to 85 percent. Even at the 70 to 85 percent level we are still

15 to 30 percent below the normal expected work pace of 100 percent.

When employees have attained our acceptable productivity performance level, then we are in the position of making other uses of our task standards. Some of these are:

1. Developing manpower budgets for our overall operation for both present and future business plans;
2. Establishing standard costs for each of our office services—this can be used for pricing these services to customers or in making decisions on the proper methods of handling these services;
3. Establishing a sounder basis for paying our employees—by either merit increases, bonus and merit, or through some form of incentive plan; and
4. Planning the future automation of clerical functions—we will be in a position to accurately weigh the cost of automation versus manual.

## Developing Manpower Budgets

Using a goal of 85 percent performance with 85 percent coverage of office activities by work measurement, you have a sound foundation upon which to base manpower budgets. You will always have some absentees and some training of new employees to consider in your overall manpower planning, so some factor must be considered to take care of this everyday event we all face. Absenteeism and training will obviously vary from area to area. For our use we will say it amounts to 15 percent of our required manpower hours.

We will use the Corporate Services Department discussed in Chapter 11 to illustrate how manpower budgets could be developed. For budgeting the manpower requirements for Corporate Services, we decide with the department head of Corporate Services that the typical work load today is 875 standard hours for the department. This corresponds to the standard hours in the last few weeks as shown on Figure 11-7 in Chapter 11.

Using this 875 standard hours as a basis, all we need to know is the anticipated increase or decrease in business for the coming year or years. If the business forecast indicates our increase will be 20 percent , then our manpower requirements will be as follows:

Basic Standard Hours Required = 875 hours + 875 hours × 20% = 875 + 175 = 1,050 hours.

$$\text{Actual Standard Hours Required} = \frac{1,050 \text{ std. hours}}{.85 \text{ perf.} \times .85 \text{ cov.}}$$

× 1.15 (for absenteeism & training) = 1,671.3 hours.

$$\text{Manpower Required} = \frac{1,671.3 \text{ hrs.}}{40 \text{ hrs/employee}} = 41.78 \text{ employees}$$

This would obviously require 42 employees, as we cannot split employees.

In referring back to Figure 11-7 in Chapter 11, you will note that in the last two weeks this department had 35 employees. If you increase this by 20 percent, you also get 42 employees. But what do you do about supervision? The above equation gave no consideration to this, because supervision would be overhead. For this example, this department would have 4 supervisors and 42 office employees budgeted.

For developing manpower budgets we can simplify our calculations if desired as follows:

$$\text{Manpower Hour Requirements Factor} = \frac{1}{\% \text{ perf.} \times \% \text{ cov.}}$$
× (1 + % abs. & trainees)

or in our example this factor would be:

$$\frac{1}{.85 \times .85} (1 + .15) = 1.384 \ (1.15) = 1.592.$$

This could, in turn, be multiplied by the 1,050 basic standard hours required to obtain the actual standard hours required, or 1,671.6. As you can see, this is within .3 hour of our detailed calculation. If desired, you could simplify your calculations. Also, the number of people would depend on the hours of your work week. Obviously, with a 37½ hour work week, more employees would be budgeted. Using 42 personnel for budget purposes, we could multiply this by the average salary per person to obtain a dollar value. For example, if the average salary for personnel in Corporate Services is $9,000/year, then our budgeted annual payroll would be $378,000, or on a monthly basis $31,500. This $31,500 could then be compared to our actual expenditures for personnel in Corporate Services each month provided business increased 20 percent as anticipated.

Even though it is anticipated that business will increase by 20 percent, the Corporate Services Department should start adding people only as increases occur. Therefore, the budget, to be meaningful, should be variable to reflect actual conditions. Based on our simplifed formula above, a variable budget could be calculated as follows:

$$\text{Variable Budget Manpower} = \frac{875\ (1 + \text{actual increase})\ 1.592}{40}$$

Variable Budget Dollars = Manpower (in whole nos.) ×

$$\frac{\$9,000}{12} = \text{Manpower} \times \$750.$$

If in the first month of the new year the business increase was only 5 percent, then the variable budget dollars would be:

$$\text{Manpower} = \frac{875\ (1 + .05)\ 1.592}{40} = 36.6 \text{ or } 37$$

Dollars = 37 × $750 = $27,750.

This would then be compared with the actual dollars spent by Corporate Services, and the difference would result in a favorable or unfavorable variance for that department.

For example, if Corporate Services had added only four personnel in the first month of the new accounting year, then this would amount to $26,250 (35 × $750). Thus the comparisons on the budget would appear as follows:

| Budgeted Payroll | Actual Payroll | Variance |
|---|---|---|
| $27,750 | $26,250 | ($1,500) |

This would indicate that Corporate Services was operating under budget which is very good, or it could be stated they had a favorable variance.

We do not wish to indicate that this is the ultimate in budgeting. This discussion is merely to illustrate some uses that can be made of standards.

## Establishing Standard Costs

A firm very often needs to know how much certain services performed in the office *actually* cost and what they *should* cost. This could be needed for costing these services to customers or for making management decisions relating to these services.

With a productivity improvement program that includes measurement, this information can be obtained by combining all the task standards involved in handling a particular service. Knowing what the various services performed in the office should cost and what they actually cost will provide valuable information for:

1. Making charges to customers for services provided—for example, banks knowing the cost of handling customers' checking accounts or lock box accounts or insurance firms handling claims for private firm, knowing the cost of claim handling, can provide a sound basis for their charges;
2. Making decisions as to how elaborate information needed for managing needs to be—very often certain statistics would be nice to have but are not really needed for de-

cision making; when the cost of these statistics is known, the statistics may actually be a luxury we cannot afford;

3.  Making decisions to automate (computerize) or use outside services for certain information—too often decisions are made to automate office activities that could not be justified from a cost point of view provided the cost were known; the same can also be true of office activities farmed out to outside services; and

4.  Making decisions on equipment purchases—too often elaborate equipment is purchased for office use that could never be justified from a cost point of view.

Knowing the costs of various services within your firm is valuable management information. Whether you maintain a standard cost system or develop one for particular situations is entirely a decision you must make.

## Establishing a Sounder Basis for Paying Employees

Several methods are available for paying employees using work measurement as the basis or as part of the plan. Some of the methods are:

1.  Using the employee's performance as a factor in merit reviews;

2.  Establishing an incentive plan for employees based on performance; or

3.  Establishing special pay or bonus plans.

Most merit rating systems are based mainly on the feelings of the employee's supervisor toward that employee as opposed to objective rating of the employee. By including the employee's performance on standards as part of the merit rating, the merit rating becomes more objective. To incorporate it into the merit rating, all you need do is add performance as another factor and reestablish the value of each factor. For example, if a perfect merit rating would be 100 points, then you may wish to redistribute these and have performance assigned 40 to 50 of the total points. To obtain the performance points, you would multiply actual average performance (say, for 13 weeks—3 months) times the 40 or 50 points. In other words, an 80 percent performer would receive 32 or 40 points, and a 60 percent performer 24 or 30 points.

If in the merit rating both the 60 percent and 80 percent performer received maximum rating on all other factors, then their ratings would be:

| *Performance* | *Rating* |
|---|---|
| 60 percent | 84 or 80 |
| 80 percent | 92 or 90 |

These would then be used as the basis for salary increases.

Before discussing incentive plans for the office, it would be well to define the true meaning of incentive payments. Incentive payments compensate an employee or employees for work performed in excess of that specified as being normal for a prescribed method, or a true incentive plan compensates employees for work in excess of normal (100 percent). Management has the responsibility of supplying the employees with sufficient work to make it possible for the employees to produce more than that normally expected. In the office this is often very difficult to do, as so much depends on customers for payments, applications, orders, deposits, etc. In other words, we must have the paper in order to work on it.

Based on the above, only a few areas in the normal office environment would be conducive to true incentive plans. That is, an incentive plan that pays the employee in direct proportion to performance over 100 percent. For the most part offices having incentive plans use an adaptation of the Halsey or Gantt profit sharing plans introduced by F. R. Halsey and H. L. Gantt in the late 1890s. These plans start the incentive payment below the 100 percent or normal level and split the increase above this level between the employee and the company.

Figure 12-1 illustrates the true incentive payment line as compared to two methods widely used in today's office incentive plans. The true incentive, as you see on Figure 12-1, is a much steeper line, but on the other two you start paying incentive at a much lower level. On an 80 percent—50/50 incentive plan (probably the most widely used), the employee is paid 1/2 percent bonus for each percent above 80 percent. At 120 percent the employee breaks even with the true (one to one) incentive and after that earns less for his or her effort.

On the 60 percent—50/50 incentive, 60 percent becomes 100 percent, and the employee is paid 1/2 percent for each 1 percent above 60 percent. This plan crosses the true incentive at 140 percent. As you can see from Figure 12-1, the employee is subsidized until 120 percent or 140 percent performance.

The reason given for normally using either the 80 percent or 60 percent incentive plan is that due to the usual low performance level in the office, it would kill all incentive to go directly to a true incentive plan. Such is also the case in many industrial situations. This is why they do not consider incentives until performance levels have reached an acceptable level. This should also be a strong consideration in the office.

Of greater importance in considering incentives in the office is providing an even work flow to employees. As you well know, this is sometimes impossible. The result is that employees who are making an effort to earn money on incentives run out of work. Being out of work can create a further problem that is misreporting which results in excessive earnings and costs. For example, J. Doe produces 100 items with a standard .030 hour/item in 2½ hours but is then out of work and waiting for 3 hours—then gets 100 more items that are produced in 2½ hours. The true performance of J. Doe

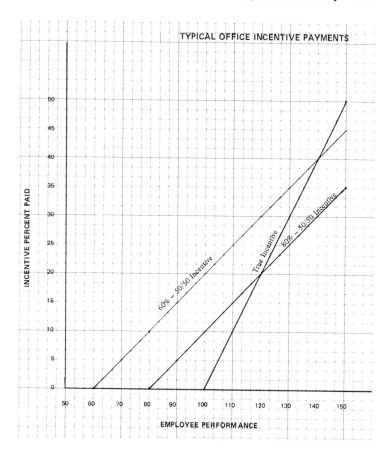

Figure 12-1

would be $(200 \times .030) \div 5$ or 120 percent. On a true incentive J. Doe would be paid for 9 hours at J. Doe's rate per hour. On the 80 percent—50/50 incentive J. Doe would receive the same amount, and on the 60 percent—50/50 incentive $5 \times 135\% + 3$ or 9.75 hours.

Suppose, for example, J. Doe reported 4 hours as waiting and 4 hours on standard. Then J. Doe's earnings would be as follows:

## SAMPLE DEPARTMENTAL BONUS CALCULATIONS

| Week Ending | Total Hours | Absent/ Loaned | Net Hours (1–2) | Standard Hours | Adjusted Standard (4 × 1.384 + 40) | % Earned (5 ÷ 3) |
|---|---|---|---|---|---|---|
| 4/18/99 | 672.0 | 40.0 | 632.0 | 275.8 | 421.7 | 66.7 |
| 4/25/99 | 660.0 | 41.5 | 618.5 | 281.4 | 429.5 | 69.4 |
| 5/2/99 | 652.0 | 42.0 | 610.0 | 280.3 | 427.9 | 70.2 |
| 5/9/99 | 625.0 | 42.0 | 583.0 | 276.9 | 423.2 | 72.6 |
| 5/16/99 | 610.0 | 31.0 | 579.0 | 284.1 | 433.2 | 74.8 |
| 5/23/99 | 600.0 | 82.5 | 517.5 | 277.5 | 424.1 | 81.9 |
| 5/30/99 | 582.0 | 65.8 | 516.2 | 281.8 | 430.0 | 83.3 |
| 6/6/99 | 560.0 | 60.0 | 500.0 | 280.3 | 427.9 | 85.6 |
| 6/13/99 | 530.0 | 40.0 | 490.0 | 282.6 | 431.1 | 88.0 |
| 6/20/99 | 530.0 | 66.5 | 463.5 | 279.4 | 426.7 | 92.1 |
| 6/27/99 | 520.0 | 44.0 | 476.0 | 281.0 | 428.9 | 90.1 |
| 7/4/99 | 484.0 | 40.0 | 444.0 | 280.0 | 427.5 | 96.2 |
| 7/11/99 | 480.0 | 32.0 | 448.0 | 282.5 | 431.0 | 96.2 |

Figure 12-2

*True Incentive* = 6 hours + 4 hours = 10 hours paid.
*80 Percent–50/50 Incentive* = 1.35 × 4 + 4 = 9.4 hours paid.
*60 Percent–50/50 Incentive* = 1.45 × 4 + 4 = 9.8 hours paid.

As you can see, this inflates earning, which in turn inflates costs, but less in the case of altered incentives as they pay more in the lower ranges. Unless you are capable of maintaining a good work flow, it is not advisable to install individual incentives.

Rather than individual incentives, you may wish to consider a bonus plan by section or department. In a section or departmental bonus plan, supervision can be included if desired. For example, suppose we decided that we would pay a bonus to all Document Processing personnel including supervision for improvements above 85 percent performance and 85 percent coverage. Then we could use our basic Weekly Performance summary report as a basis for calculating if any bonus is due, as shown on Figure 12-2.

## chapter thirteen

# An Ideal Productivity Improvement Situation

NO OFFICE WILL EVER have a truly ideal productivity improvement situation. However, you will be surprised how close you may come to similar situations in your own office area if you approach your productivity improvement program correctly.

## The Situation

In our ideal situation we find the following in our Order Entry (manufacturing), Policy Application (insurance), or Loan Application (banks) sections:

1. Orders or applications are received in sealed envelopes by five clerks in batches of 50 ten times per day by each clerk.

2. Each clerk checks each of the orders or applications to make sure it is complete. This involves reading a full name, street address, city, state and zip code, and the average of six lines consisting of five words and two 5-digit numbers per line. Incomplete orders (those with missing information) are put in one pile and complete ones in another pile—with an average of 5 incompletes per batch of 50. Both completes and incompletes are put in alphabetical order.

3. Incompletes are given to the supervisor who contacts the originator by telephone to obtain missing information. This involves calling one area office for each of the five clerks. After the supervisor completes the missing information, documents are returned to clerks.

4. On the complete documents the clerk enters price of each item ordered from a price book on orders. The clerk enters on applications from rate book the normal premium or loan percentage for the type insurance or loan applied for. Documents are then placed in manila envelopes, addressed to an individual, and placed in "out" basket. When incompletes are returned, they are handled in the same manner.

5. Later, average daily is same as number sent out. Orders or applications are returned in manila envelope to clerks. Orders/applications are then checked for approval/disapproval with average of 1 per 50 being disapproved, and disapproved orders/applications are given to the supervisor.

6. The supervisor contacts area office for each of the disapproved orders/applications and tells the manager who was disapproved and why and then returns disapproved orders to clerks.

7. Each clerk enters the approved orders/applications in a journal with name and address of applicant and total

amount of order/policy/loan. Page is totaled, tape torn off, and asided. Orders/applications are then totaled and tape compared to previous tape. If tapes agree, total is entered on journal page. If totals are not the same, both tapes are checked, corrections made, and total posted. This occurs on an average of once per 20 days.

8. After posting, orders/applications are sent to next department in manila envelope with tape containing total. Disapproved orders are sent to area office in another envelope.

9. At the end of the day each clerk totals the 10 pages in the journal, checks total, and enters it on a daily log which is turned over to the supervisor.

10. The supervisor copies total for each area on area daily report and places report in pre-addressed envelope and asides it in "out" basket on desk—five reports per day.

All employees and the supervisor of this section are very cooperative in discussing the work in detail. The section was measured as described above with the standard per order or application being .0134 hour.

Prior to measurement, this section worked an average of 10 hours per day to get out the work load of 2,500 orders/applications per day ($50 \times 10 \times 5$). After the measurement was installed, they gradually reduced overtime to a normal 8 hours/day to produce the 2,500 orders/applications. With an average pay per hour of $7.00, the cost per item produced was $.154 prior to measurement [$7 (50 hours + 5 hours premium) ÷ 2,500 orders/application]. After reduction to 40 hours per employee the cost dropped to $.112 per item. This resulted in a savings of $.042 per item ($.154 − $.112).

The checking for missing information by the supervisor required on the average 1 minute per order/application. The reporting of disapproved orders was found to require 2 minutes per order/application.

Assuming that this is all that was done by this section, the section averaged with five people working 8 hours each per day 83.8 percent on standards (2,500 items × 0.134 hours/ item ÷ 40 hours). The supervisor in turn spent some 350 minutes out of the day handling the incomplete and disapproved orders by telephone. This meant that 72.9 percent (350 minutes ÷ 480 minutes) of an hour/day was spent on the telephone. This left only 130 minutes per day to supervise the five clerks, or some 26 minutes per clerk.

Even though the clerks improved their performance with measurement during interviews they all expressed the desire to have more contact with the area office that each served. Nothing was done to provide for this in the basic study that was implemented. Later on it was decided that some action would be taken to free the supervisor to spend more time supervising this section as well as another section of the same size with similar work.

## Situation With Motivation

In the situation just discussed, the principles of redesigning jobs to better motivate employees were combined with the work measurement. To accomplish this both the work measurement analyst and supervision were introduced to the principle of motivation through a simple training course entitled "Job Design for Motivation," as outlined on Figure 13-1. This course requires approximately 32 hours for the average supervisor or work measurement analyst.

Following the basic training the supervisor, work measurement analyst, and employees discussed positive changes that could be made to provide more challenge to the employees in doing their work. These sessions resulted in each employee being assigned more responsibility for handling his or her service area.

| JOB DESIGN FOR MOTIVATION | COURSE OUTLINE | January 1980 Page 1 of 2 |
|---|---|---|

| Lesson Number | Code | Lesson Title |
|---|---|---|
| 1 | AUDIO-700 | An Introduction to Job Design for Motivation |
| 2 | REF-707 | Objectives and Terminology |
| 3 | REF-701 | The Basics of Work Motivation Theory |
| 4 | PI-705 | The Motivation — Maintenance Theory |
| 5 | REF-703 | Textbook Reading Assignments |
| 6 | TEXT | Reading Assignment — Chapter 1, The Problem |
| 7 | PI-716 | Finding Jobs That Need Redesign for Motivation |
| 8 | RcF-719 | Industrial Engineering and Job Design for Motivation |
| 9 | RT-704 | Addressing the Problem |
| 10 | AUDIO-725 | Case Study - Treasury Department |
| 11 | TEXT | Reading Assignment — Chapter 4, What Motivates? |
| 12 | REF-721 | What About Incentives? |
| 13 | PI-702 | How To Bring About Changes in Employee Behavior |
| 14 | TEXT | Reading Assignment — Chapter 5, Redesigning Jobs for Motivation |
| 15 | AV-710 | Why Jobs Die |
| 16 | RT-708 | Keeping Jobs Alive |
| 17 | AUDIO-706 | Job Enrichment Lessons From AT&T |
| 18 | TEXT | Reading Assignment — Chapter 6, Maintaining the Motivation |
| 19 | PI-712 | Case Study (Greenlight Session) — Keypunch Operator |
| 20 | AV-727 | The Supervisor's Job |
| 21 | TEXT | Reading Assignment — Chapter 7, The Quiet Revolution |
| 22 | RT-724 | Keeping Motivation Maintained |
| 23 | AUDIO-723 | The Key Person Is Essential to Success |
| 24 | PI-713 | Case Study (Greenlight Session) — Bagmaking Machine |
| 25 | TEXT | Reading Assignment, Appendix Case 1 — Telephone Directory Compilation |
| 26 | AUDIO-730 | Greenlight Session — Engineering Records Clerk |
| 27 | TEXT | Reading Assignment, Appendix Case 2 — Typewriter Assembly Line |
| 28 | REF-722 | The Art of Reshaping Jobs |
| 29 | AUDIO-720 | Greenlight Session — Automobile Insurance Department |
| 30 | AV-729 | How Does Job Design for Motivation Reduce Costs? |
| 31 | TEXT | Reading Assignment, Appendix Case 3 — The Long Distance Frameman's Job |

Figure 13-1 (Cont. on following page)

An individual with behavioral science training acted as moderator at the meetings between the supervisor, work measurement analysts, and employees. The purpose of the moderator was to make sure the discussion sessions did not take any negative trends. These sessions are similar to brainstorming and no idea is allowed to be criticized. The meetings are referred to as "greenlighting."

| JOB DESIGN FOR MOTIVATION | COURSE OUTLINE | January 1980 Page 2 of 2 |
|---|---|---|
| Lesson Number | Code | Lesson Title |

| Lesson Number | Code | Lesson Title |
|---|---|---|
| 32 | PI-718 | High Level Motivation for Low Level Occupations |
| 33 | AUDIO-731 | Greenlight Session — Adjustment Section |
| 34 | REF-728 | Job Design and the Unions |
| 35 | AUDIO-726 | Help From the Exit Interview |
| 36 | TEST | Final Review |

© 1980 Training Techniques Company, Inc.

**Figure 13-1 (cont.)**

Before discussing the results of these sessions, why not jot down on a piece of paper what you would consider doing from the list of ideas created from the first "greenlighting" session. Figure 13-2 contains the ideas recorded. Write on a sheet of paper the number opposite each idea and record next to this number what you would do or not do.

Items 1 and 2 were not considered as really important

|  | Do | Not Do |
|---|---|---|
| 1. Improve the decor and lighting of the work area for the clerks. | ___ | ___ |
| 2. Provide each clerk with private office area. | ___ | ___ |
| 3. Let each clerk call the area that he/she served to complete the orders/applications. | ___ | ___ |
| 4. Let one clerk have the responsibility for calling the areas to complete the orders/applications. | ___ | ___ |
| 5. Let each clerk call the area served to report disapproved orders/applications. | ___ | ___ |
| 6. Let one clerk call the areas served to report disapproved orders/applications. | ___ | ___ |
| 7. Let each clerk prepare and mail daily reports to the areas and give the supervisor a copy for preparing summary reports. | ___ | ___ |
| 8. Assign present work done by supervisor to the clerks as a group and let them decide how to handle the calls and reports. | ___ | ___ |

**Figure 13-2**

when the final results came in. These two items are what the behavioral scientist refers to as hygiene. Items 3, 5, and 7 were selected and implemented. After implementaion, the standard per item was .0157 hour including the calls to the areas. The five clerks still handled the 2,500 items per day in 8 hours per clerk. This resulted in an overall performance of 98.1 percent.

Business increased, and the number of orders/applications averaged 60 per batch per clerk, or 3,000 per day. This obviously would require the clerks either working well over 100 percent (normal work pace) to complete the orders in 8 hours/day or result in overtime. The clerks requested a meeting with supervision and suggested they receive additional pay if they completed the orders/applications in 8 hours with good quality.

Supervision took this up with work measurement, and the two decided to present an incentive plan to top management for paying the clerks in direct proportion to their increase over 100 percent. The standard of .0157 hour/item was audited and found sound for use in the proposed incentive plan. Management approved the plan, and it was implemented.

The five clerks produced the 3,000 items in 8 hours per day per clerk at an acceptable quality level. This resulted in each clerk being paid 17.8 percent more per hour. Based on the $7/hour previously discussed, this meant each employee was now making $8.25/hour. This pleased the employees, but management began to wonder about costs.

Based on the standard of .0157 hour/item times 3,000 items/day, the hours required would be 47.1 hours/day. At 100 percent performance and no lost time, this would require six employees without incentives. Six employees working 8 hours/day at $7/hour each would cost $336 as compared to $329.70 paid five employees to handle the work on incentive—a savings of $6.30/day plus the normal fringe benefits paid employees. With fringe benefits being in excess of 30 percent of salary, management was satisfied the incentive was in the best interest of both the company and the employees.

In addition to the above comparison, management was also reminded that 2,500 items were handled in the beginning by five employees and a full-time supervisor working 10 hours each per day. With both receiving overtime premium and supervision being paid $9/hour, the cost per item in the beginning was $.1936 [(55 hours × $7/hour + 11 hours × $9/hour) ÷ 2,500 items]. The present method required only half-time (4 hours/day) of the supervisor. Therefore, present cost per item was $.1219 [(47.1 hours × $7/hour + 4 hours × $9/hour) ÷ 3,000 items]. The difference in these costs is $.0717/item or a savings of $215.10/day ($.0717/item × 3,000 items/day).

This example is obviously an ideal one, as it has not considered any absenteeism, vacation time, or turnover of employees. Even so, it does illustrate what can happen when employees are motivated to perform the work required.

## chapter fourteen

# Continuing Your Productivity Improvement Program

AS YOU ARE IMPLEMENTING your productivity improvement program, business grows so as to fully utilize your existing staff. Due to the efforts of the program, the productivity of your staff increases from a 60 percent level to an 80 percent level. Everyone in management is well pleased with the results; however, they see no need to continue the cost of a productivity improvement staff and the reporting and controls, and both are gradually eliminated. Sound familiar? It is often very familiar to firms, and this is why so many productivity improvement programs ultimately fail.

No matter whether your productivity improvement program is based on a behavioral science or an industrial engineering approach, or a combination of both, it requires continuous attention to provide lasting results. This attention is better known as maintenance of the program and without it, the productivity improvements made will ultimately be lost. The employees will soon slip back into old habits without attention from management as to how each employee or group of employees is progressing. A large part of any productivity improvement program is recognition and appreciation by peers and superiors of a job well-done. When this no longer exists, the desire to do a good job wanes.

Changes that occur within firms in relation to equipment, forms, etc., are another reason you must continue to maintain your productivity improvement program. Since your firm is not static, neither is your productivity or the program to keep it going at an acceptable pace.

How do you properly maintain a productivity improvement program that is operating successfully? The answer must be made by another question, "What do you consider successful?" If your goal in your productivity improvement program was to reach an average of 80 percent performance with a minimum of 85 percent coverage, then you might say your program is successful when reports indicate you are attaining this week after week. This sounds great, but our labor costs do not stay static nor do our fringe benefits. So what we must constantly strive for is improving productivity to offset wage and fringe benefit increases.

To keep abreast of our ever-increasing costs of wages and fringe benefits, we must continue to properly maintain our productivity improvement program and look for ways to further improve productivity in line with costs. For example, if we handled 10,000 checks, policies, or orders per week with 200 office employees working 40 hours each per week at $7/hour with fringe benefits amounting to 30 percent of salary, our cost in labor per check, policy, or order would be $7.28 [(200 employees × 40 hours/week/employee × $7/hour × 1.30 fringes) ÷ 10,000 checks/policies/orders]. If through our productivity improvement program we produced this same quantity with 160 employees (this is an average reduction from a sound program), then our cost per check, policy, or order would be $5.824, or a reduction of $1.176 per check, policy, or order.

Even if we decided to share this savings with the employees by increasing their base pay to $7.70 per hour (10 percent), our cost per check, policy, or order would be only $6.4064, or a savings of $.8736 per check, policy, or order as compared to our original cost. As increases are made in the future, this savings will eventually disappear, and costs will eventually exceed the one prior to productivity improvement. True, you may be able to increase the cost of checks, policies, or orders to offset the increased labor costs, but you will ultimately find that you are not competitive. Such is the case that many of our firms face today in competition—especially with foreign products.

To stay competitive means proper maintenance and continuous improvement in productivity. Maintenance involves the following:

1. Constant auditing of reporting and controls in each area covered by measurement:
2. Periodic review of each area with supervision to ascertain any changes that may have occurred;
3. Periodic discussions with supervision and employees relating to improvements that should be considered;
4. Review of rquests for new or revised equipment to supply data to justify change;
5. Review of requests for personnel additions to make sure they can be properly justified;
6. Review of system and procedures changes planned to aid in their justification and impact on productivity; and
7. Provide assistance as required in cost problems.

As you see, your productivity improvement personnel will have plenty to do after implementation of the basic program.

We will now discuss some of the important factors in each of these.

## Auditing of Reporting and Controls

No matter how your firm determined the time required to perform a given amount of work, the reports showing how an individual or group is performing are valuable in maintaining your program. To determine how they can be used, let us discuss Figure 14-1.

As you can see, Figure 14-1 is a Weekly Performance Summary Report for the Data Entry Section of the Computer Services Department. You will note that for the first five weeks shown, coverage was at 85 to 90 percent, and performance at 85 to 92 percent for the 10 Data Entry Operators. In the sixth week coverage dropped to 83 percent, in the seventh to 80 percent and finally in the thirteenth week to 70 percent, with performance remaining about the same. You

WEEKLY PERFORMANCE SUMMARY REPORT

| DEPARTMENT Computer Services | | | | SECTION Data Entry | | | | CCC | SUPERVISOR John Smythe | |
|---|---|---|---|---|---|---|---|---|---|---|
| WEEK ENDING | TOTAL EMPLOYEES ASSIGNED | HOURS | | | | | | | % COVERAGE | % PERFORMANCE |
| | | TOTAL | ABSENT/ LOANED | SUPERVISORY | UNMEASURED | | ACTUAL | STANDARD | | |
| | | | | | NO STANDARD | OTHER | | | | |
| 4-18-99 | 10 | 400.0 | 8.0 | 40.0 | 29.1 | 6.1 | 316.8 | 291.5 | 90 | 92 |
| 4-25-99 | 10 | 400.0 | – | 40.0 | 32.0 | 7.6 | 320.4 | 278.7 | 89 | 87 |
| 5-2-99 | 10 | 400.0 | 6.0 | 40.0 | 30.2 | 12.3 | 311.5 | 268.1 | 88 | 86 |
| 5-9-99 | 10 | 400.0 | 8.0 | 40.0 | 30.4 | 8.3 | 313.3 | 269.3 | 89 | 86 |
| 5-16-99 | 10 | 400.0 | 8.0 | 40.0 | 34.3 | 18.5 | 299.2 | 254.3 | 85 | 85 |
| 5-23-99 | 10 | 400.0 | 8.0 | 40.0 | 34.2 | 25.6 | 292.2 | 263.0 | 83 | 90 |
| 5-30-99 | 10 | 400.0 | 16.0 | 40.0 | 30.6 | 38.2 | 275.2 | 244.9 | 80 | 89 |
| 6-6-99 | 10 | 400.0 | 8.0 | 40.0 | 34.2 | 39.7 | 278.1 | 236.4 | 79 | 85 |
| 6-13-99 | 10 | 400.0 | – | 40.0 | 33.4 | 67.4 | 259.2 | 220.3 | 72 | 85 |
| 6-20-99 | 10 | 400.0 | 8.0 | 40.0 | 34.3 | 64.3 | 253.4 | 217.9 | 72 | 86 |
| 6-27-99 | 10 | 400.0 | 16.0 | 40.0 | 33.6 | 66.2 | 244.2 | 212.5 | 71 | 87 |
| 7-4-99 | 10 | 400.0 | 8.0 | 40.0 | 34.4 | 71.2 | 246.4 | 216.8 | 70 | 88 |
| 7-11-99 | 10 | 400.0 | – | 40.0 | 34.4 | 73.6 | 252.0 | 214.2 | 70 | 85 |

COMMENTS

| ISSUED BY C. Campbell, Mgr., Work Measurement | DATE 7-13-99 |
|---|---|

Figure 14-1

will also note on Figure 14-1 that "unmeasured other" is now in the 64 to 74 hour per week range. This indicates that a lot of "no work available" is occurring.

On investigating the Data Entry Section, we find that volume received and processed per week has been gradually declining for five weeks, but the supervisor assures us that this is temporary. We then investigate why volume has fallen and find that several areas of our firm have gone on-line for Data Entry. This means that these areas now enter data directly in the computer and no longer need to use Data Entry. This immediately indicates that Data Entry's staffing needs reviewing as do the standards for the departments now online. The result is that ultimately Data Entry will require two less people, and the areas that went on-line some three less people. Standards for both areas require revision.

Another key way performance reports such as Figure 14-1 can indicate changes is by performance gradually climbing with coverage remaining almost constant. This is a definite indication that methods have changed making the present standards no longer valid. With no incentives or form of bonus being paid, a danger signal is indicated when a section's average performance is over 100 percent. With incentives or a bonus plan, overall section averages above 130 percent normally deserve investigation.

## Periodic Review With Supervision

This is well worthwhile as it indicates to supervision that you are interested in his or her area. If approached correctly, it can reveal difficulties that will be encountered which can be planned for as well as changes that will ultimately require revision of standards.

For example, on such a periodic review with the Mail Section of Office Services, the supervisor discussed a mail campaign that Sales had asked them to handle. The campaign would involve folding inserts twice, placing them in envelopes, running the envelopes through the postage meter, sorting them by zip code, bundling them, and placing the banded items in mail bags. The project would involve 5,000 pieces, and the supervisor didn't have any idea how long it would take.

The productivity improvement group aided the supervisor in estimating the time, and they came up with 19.4 hours required at 100 percent performance. The supervisor then asked how long it would take at 70 percent and 90 percent performance. The supervisor explained that part-time employees had averaged 70 percent while full-time employees had been averaging 90 percent. The supervisor wanted to be able to compare the cost of part-time help at $10 per hour versus using full-time personnel on overtime.

The productivity improvement group assisted in this calculation and brought up a factor that the supervisor did not think of. That is, no fringes are paid on part-time help, but they are on full-time help. Based on the average cost of $7 per hour in the Mail Section, the comparison came out as shown on Figure 14-2.

$$\text{Part-time Cost} = \frac{19.4}{.70} \times \$10 = \qquad \$277.14$$

$$\text{Full-time Cost} = \frac{19.4}{.90} \times \$10.50 \times 1.30 = \qquad 294.23$$

$$\text{Savings using Part-Time} = \qquad \$17.09$$

NOTE:  $10.50 is overtime rate per hour.

**Figure 14-2. Cost Comparison**

Besides this kind of assistance, you will often find that changes are being considered in the supervisor's area that will ultimately affect standards and staffing. You will improve relations and the productivity of personnel by aiding prior to changes actually taking place.

## Periodic Discussions With Supervisors and Personnel

This is merely combining the previous discussions with those held with personnel in the area. This should be done with the full agreement of the supervisor.

By talking with the employees, you often find that changes have taken place gradually which may or may not have an impact on the standards. Again, you indicate and interest which is well worthwhile from a morale point of view and very often are given suggestions for improving the operations.

After all, no one knows a job better than the person performing it.

## Review of Requests for New or Revised Equipment

It is amazing how much new or revised equipment is purchased by firms on impulse or to keep up with the Joneses. The key to the purchase of any equipment is the need for the selected equipment to adequately do the job required.

You need a printing calculator for multiplying, dividing, adding, and subtracting in your office. In talking with various firms supplying calculators of the type needed, you find that for only $20 more you can get special features that may someday be useful. So you purchase the special feature model. So what, you are probably saying—$20 is peanuts. True, but in a large firm this $20 can pyramid into a five or six digit figure very rapidly, as each person requiring a calculator will want the special model.

By properly using your productivity improvement group, you can have them gather all the information needed on which to decide what you should or should not buy. Once Purchasing has the basic data on the cost, size, capacity, etc., of various pieces of equipment, then true comparisons can be made. You may also save yourself some embarrassing and costly maintenance work.

To illustrate the meaning of this last statement, a firm the author has worked with decided on impulse that they would purchase a special duplicator to reproduce some special forms that were costly to print in small quantities. The duplicator was installed in the main office area with all personnel in that area present for the training. Everything went fine during the demonstration and training. Later in the day some form copies were needed and the duplicator was turned on. All the lights went out. Unfortunately, the warm-up power required for the duplicator overloaded the electrical circuits when other equipment was operating. The net result was the installation of a special circuit for the duplicator—not an inexpensive item.

Of just as much importance in the previous example is the inflexibility of layout created by having a piece of equipment that can be placed in only one location. Flexibility is a necessity today in the office area. You must be in a position to arrange your office to properly utilize your personnel as business needs require.

When purchasing new or revised equipment, evaluate it from a cost point of view as well as:

1. What is needed to handle the present business requirements as well as those of the foreseeable future;
2. What kind of service is available for properly maintaining the equipment—the most elaborate equipment is of no value to you when you must wait for days or weeks to have it repaired;
3. How does the equipment compare in cost of operation to your present or other equipment being considered—if the equipment is expensive, this is an important consideration;
4. How portable is the equipment—does it require special electrical connections, venting, etc.; and

5. What space requirements are truly needed to operate the equipment—consider both the space needed for the equipment and supplies for its operation.

These are not all of the items that should be investigated, but they should start you on developing your own checklist.

## Review of Requests for Personnel Additions

Your productivity improvement group should not have the power to deny personnel additions. They should review all such requests and make recommendations as to whether or not the additional personnel are needed. Having them review requests is also a means of alerting them to review the work being performed in the area requesting additional personnel.

Often changes have occurred in the area that may or may not require the requested additional personnel. By reviewing the area, you can determine if the additional personnel are truly needed. Perhaps by making some changes in the way work is done, present personnel can handle the changed conditions. At any rate, the requests are a method of alerting your productivity improvement group that a review may be in order.

## Review of System and Procedure Changes

If your productivity improvement group is not part of your systems and procedures department, a sound line of communications should be established. By having the two fully cooperate, you will reduce the resistance to changes that always occur when systems and procedures are revised. You will also reduce the number of revisions needed to ensure sound operation of a new system or procedure. Changes anticipated in systems and procedures always affect the work required to handle paper. With good communications be-

tween productivity improvement and systems and procedures, preparation of new standards can take place prior to
the actual implementation of a new or revised system or procedure.

Meaning no disrespect to the systems oriented personnel,
they are usually not good communicators. This is due to their
training and approach to their work. However, a combination
of system oriented and work measurement oriented personnel provides for a smooth transition from the drawing
board to actual implementation.

By having these two disciplines working closely, you will
eliminate a great deal of the so-called "mystique" of automating operations. You will also be basing your anticipated
savings through automation on more realistic estimates. Far
too often the fact that information must be fed into the system is overlooked as well as the most economical and practical
method of gathering the information.

## Provide Assistance as Required in Costing

Very often management needs to compare the cost of handling certain functions internally versus having the functions
handled by an outside supplier. Your productivity improvement group would be an excellent source for supplying you
with the information on which to make such a decision.

Many of the activities in the office are necessary due to the
kind of business in which your firm is operating. Some of
these necessary services are performed as a service to others
and in doing so, you need to know your cost of these services.
For example, it is not unusual for an insurance company to
handle claims for a self-insured firm, a bank to handle payment of bills (lock box), or a manufacturing firm to handle a
customer's material. The days of doing this "for free" and
staying in business are no longer around, but you must price
these properly to be competitive.

In many firms with which your author is familiar, the vast number of reports generated would be greatly reduced if the cost of producing them were truly known. Some we have found that may parallel a condition you have that has gone unnoticed are:

1. Manual consolidation of a series of computer-generated reports—if needed at all, the chances are it could be created far cheaper by the computer;
2. Rearranging information in a different format to fit a particular group or executive's needs—this usually happens where information is available but not in the format a particular executive desires;
3. Creating special reports from existing reports—this normally occurs in firms which have expanded into different lines than previously handled, and special formulae are used to equate all items to the original product line—often meaningless, but if required, could probably be handled more cheaply by a computer; and
4. Continuation of reports that are no longer of value to anyone—this is usually the result of a top executive requesting a special report and not emphasizing the fact that it is not to be a continuous activity.

Why not look at your operation and find out which of the reports you receive are truly useful to you in doing your job. It may surprise you to find that there are quite a few. Even more surprising, you may find that often no one else who receives them actually needs them to do his or her job well.

Requesting reports and being on the list of those receiving them have to some degree become a part of the prestige of being in management. How many of your reports are actually worth the cost of their preparation? Why not find out?

chapter fifteen

# The Computer and Productivity Improvement

THERE IS LITTLE DOUBT the computer has had a major impact on the way we do business. Without it we would be lost in a mass of perpetually incomplete detail. Although we agree that the computer has definitely improved our mode of business operation, the question exists as to whether we have utilized the computer or the computer has utilized us.

For instance, very often we hear, as a reason for not making changes, "We cannot do it that way, as our computer programs will not accept it." What is really being said is, "If we make that change, we will have to either revise or rewrite our computer software program."

True, this excuse is becoming less and less of a reason for making changes. In fact, computer programs are far more flexible today and more useful to management. Take, for example, the computer software for work measurement. At first you either bought a particular work measurement system in its entirety or the software was not useful to your firm. There is little doubt that software to handle your office work measurement, reporting, and costing is valuable. However, we are going to discuss here what you should look for in such software rather than a particular software package such as that offered by the author's firm, known as MCD-MOD-II.

The things to look for in computer software for use in measuring office work are:

1. Will the basic data file take any kind of office standard data;
2. Can the basic data file be updated as changes occur;
3. Will updated data in the basic data file automatically trigger an updating of standards containing the old data;
4. Will the software permit expansion of the basic file in a logical manner as conditions require;
5. Can task standards be revised with a minimum input and yet maintain a record of all revisions;
6. Can standards on file be used to establish similar standards without affecting the original standard;
7. Can allowances be varied to fit differing conditions that may exist;
8. Can preliminary task data be stored without a printout and later updated to fit actual conditions;
9. Can elements tailored for activities in your firm be properly stored and utilized when needed; and
10. Can existing task standards be used to create standards for comparing methods without affecting the existing task standard?

These are but a few of the features a software package should have to be useful. So you will understand their importance, we will now discuss each feature.

## Flexible Basic Data File

If you have an up-to-date work measurement productivity improvement program based on the work measurement approach you feel best fits your needs, then you need a computer software package that will accept your approach. You do not need a software package that requires you to utilize a different work measurement approach. When considering any of the software packages, be sure the package will accept your data and does not require you to change to an approach that fits the software.

Even though your present task standards have all been prepared manually, it is far more economical to convert existing standards over to the computer. It can become costly to completely redo the standards with a different data base. Even if some standards need updating, utilizing your present approach for this updating will be more economical in most cases than using a new approach. The only way a new approach can be justified is when an existing approach is obsolete and is no longer economical to use.

Another important reason for making sure the software has a flexible data file is realizing that in the future you may need to update this data file. After all, equipment, systems, and methods are constantly improving, and your data file must be capable of handling these improvements. Some advocates will tell you that data does not change enough to warrant this flexibility. Do not let them hoodwink you with this, as all approaches must be continuously researched and updated to properly measure changes that are constantly occurring.

For example, typewriters have gone from predominantly manual to electric to selectric to word processing in a relatively short time. Adding machines, as such, are almost unheard of, yet some ten years ago they were the vogue. Therefore, the data file must be flexible to permit updating as well as utilization of the standard data that best fits today's needs.

## Updating Capability

From our discussion above it is obvious that a flexible data file should permit updating in the future. This is not always the case with all software packages that will accept most standard data approaches. Some packages can be tailored to accept your favorite data, but once they are placed on file, you will not be able to make any changes without assistance from the software vendor. Make sure that the software you select permits you to update your data as required without the need of outside assistance.

"Why is this important?" you may be asking. It is important because your task standards cannot be kept up to date unless you have the capability of updating the data file. Make sure you have this updating capability and that it will trigger automatically the updating of standards. The updating of the data file may exist in a software package, but it may not contain the program steps to automatically update existing standards. This feature is probably the most important of all in utilizing a computer for work measurement.

## Automatic Standard Update

Have you ever updated a task standard due to an equipment change and wondered how many more task standards would be affected by this change? If you have been involved in work measurement for any length of time, you have encountered this feeling. No doubt you remembered quite a number of them and possibly all and finally updated all of them. It could have been handled very simply by a computer software package that would have automatically updated all task standards containing the updated element or elements, so be sure the software package you consider has this feature.

Of all features, the automatic standard update is probably the most economically justified for utilizing the computer for work measurement. To illustrate, suppose your firm is updating your word processing equipment and going from equipment capable of 150-6 inch lines per minute to 300-6 inch lines per minute. To make this change all you need do is replace the present time of .0067 minute with the new time of .0033 minute in the software data file. This change should then automatically generate updated standards for all tasks containing the revised element.

Your next problem could be that only part of word processing is converting to the new equipment. If this is the case, with the proper software this will not be a problem, as the previous standards are kept on file. If the above revision were the first since standards were established, all you need do is to instruct those using the old word processing equipment to use a dash (–) and a zero (0) after the task code. This would automatically tell you that the original task should be used for reporting and controls.

## Basic Data File Expansion

One of the features of using a computer to assist in work measurement is that of being able to tailor data to measure common elements. To accomplish this properly, you must be able to develop elements that are tailored to your needs and place them in the basic data file. Make sure the software you are considering has this capability.

Also, make sure the capability is not that of just an add-on type. It should provide you with the capability of integrating your special data in the proper area of the data file. This means that the file must be of an indexed and direct access nature. Obviously expansion of the basic data file will increase storage requirements, but this expansion must not increase computer usage time searching for the needed data.

## Minimum Task Standard Revision Input

It goes without saying that you do not wish to overload the memory storage of your computer. You can keep all standards stored on tape or a removable disc. As needed, the tape or disc can be placed on-line. Once on-line, you need the capability of calling up present standards and revising only the items that have changed.

Once you have revised the changed items, then you can either obtain a hard copy of the resulting standard and task description or almost immediately read and record the resulting standard time.

For maintaining a proper record of revisions, you will need to have a hard copy of the original standard and each revision in a file or have the original and each revision kept on file in the computer. It would be well to have the computer maintain the file and periodically print out obsolete standards and drop them from the computer file. This would provide a more foolproof method of maintaining a proper history of standards.

## Using Existing Standards To Establish New Standards

In all work measurement certain tasks are the same except for some pecularities due to flow of paper, work content, or the basic work area. It is often possible to use an existing standard to establish a new standard. In doing this you do not want in any way to affect the existing standard. You can easily do this with properly structured software. All that is normally required, if the software is properly structured, is to use the existing standard as input for the new standard.

Suppose, for example, that the job preparation, work performed, and job wrap-up are the same for a new task being measured except for frequencies. Then with the proper software, you should be able to use the task standard on file as input to create the new standard. To do this all you need do is enter the new task code, task name, and other pecularities different from those of the standard on file. The result should be a new task standard with no reference to the existing task standard or in no way affecting the existing task standard.

## Variable Allowances

As we discussed in an earlier chapter, allowances for personal time, rest periods, and short (unavoidable) delays may vary from firm to firm or even from one office area to another. Therefore, computer software for work measurement should provide for changing allowances as conditions demand.

Do not be taken in by the sales pitch that the national average for allowances should be sufficient for any firm. This is a great idea, but your firm is not *any* firm.

The average allowance is 15 percent, which is the equivalent of 63 minutes lost per day in an 8-hour (480 minute) day. If your firm works only 7 hours (420 minutes) per day and you still need to allow for 63 minutes lost, your allowance should be 17.6 percent or 18 percent, and not 15 percent. As you can see, you must be able to vary conditions.

## Storing Preliminary Data

To properly utilize the computer in work measurement, you must be able to place preliminary data on file and later finalize it into a task standard or standards. The software you select must permit this capability or you will accomplish only a small portion of the reduction of detailed work on the part of the analyst.

While storing preliminary data, the software must also provide the capability of storing information of benefit to work measurement personnel but meaningless to users of standards. For examples, very often it is good to explain how a frequency was arrived at so standards can be properly maintained in the future. A good software package will provide for this and print out this information only on the task step detail.

An important use of preliminary data is to finalize the best method for performing a task. The preliminary work can be used to sell supervision and the employees on the benefits of the best method. Once the method is accepted, then the preliminary data can be finalized and placed on file as a standard.

## Storage of Tailored Elements

Combining several elements into larger elements for measuring specific activities in the office area will reduce the time required to measure work and often results in more consistent standards. After all, this is the philosophy of standard data development. Nearly every standard data approach for measuring office work available today ignores this important feature of standard data to a large degree. Almost every firm that sells an office work measurement approach gives you the impression that their approach is the ultimate. The writer's firm is no exception.

Basically, the various office work measurement approaches available are similar to a large degree. None of those available, including the approach of the author's firm, will solve all your work measurement problems in the office area. There is no way a "canned answer" can be developed for each condition encountered in the office.

The result is that your firm will need the capability of adding special data to any software you may acquire. The software should provide you with alternate methods of storing this tailored data. The alternates should be by adding to the data file of the basic software package or storing it in a special area of your standards file. Data tailored to your firm's needs that is usable in all office areas should be stored in the basic software data file. On the other hand, data that is applicable only to certain areas should be stored in a special section of your standards file.

The key is whether or not the software package has this capability. Some will, but the majority will not, as the "canned data" is supposed to be the ultimate.

## Using Existing Task Standards To Create Standards for Methods Comparisons

Have you ever prepared a cost justification for buying or leasing new equipment? If so, then one of the major factors is the saving in labor costs. More often than not this labor saving is a rough estimate based on a few key operations that will be principally impacted by the new equipment. In fringe cases, having the impact of the new equipment across the board could be the deciding factor to buy or not to buy.

With properly structured software, you can find out every task that will be affected by the new equipment and the increase or decrease in task time that will result. Properly handled, you can continue all standards "as is" or quickly update them when the new equipment is installed.

Have you ever thought about a way to improve a particular job but never got around to evaluating the value of the improvement? Normally you did not get around to the evaluation because of the time required to rework standards manually to determine the savings potential. With properly structured computer software, this can be easily done without affecting any of the existing standards and in a minimum of time on your part.

## Summary

This chapter really serves two purposes. The first is to get you to think about what you really need in computer software to assist in productivity improvement. The second is to, hopefully, convince you that you should develop what you want from software and then look for the software that will fit your needs. Too often software is obtained that does not truly serve the needs of the user.

# appendix a

# MCD-MOD-I

## MASTER CLERICAL DATA MOD-I

Do not attempt to use this chart unless you understand the proper application of the data. This statement is included as a word of caution to prevent difficulties resulting from misapplication.

Copyright © 1977
by

**SERGE A. BIRN COMPANY**
Division of SABCO Inc.

Management Consultants

LOUISVILLE • NEW YORK • FT. LAUDERDALE • LONDON (MARLOW)

Affiliates

MELBOURNE • FRANKFURT • DUBLIN

### A — ARRANGE PAPERS

| | | |
|---|---|---|
| COLLATE | | |
| TWO SHEETS | ACT | 42 |
| ADD'L SHEETS | ACA | 27 |
| SORT | | |
| GROUPS | ASG | 47 |
| PIGEONHOLES | ASP | 69 |
| ALPHABETICALLY | | |
| 0 THRU 19 | ASA01 | 72 |
| 20 THRU 29 | ASA02 | 79 |
| OVER 30 | ASA03 | 85 |

### B — BODY ELEMENTS

| | | |
|---|---|---|
| ARISE AND SIT | BAS | 208 |
| SEATED TURN | BST | 122 |
| BEND AND ARISE | BBA | 61 |
| WALK PER STEP | BW6 | 17 |

### C — CALCULATE

| | | |
|---|---|---|
| ELECTRONICALLY | | |
| ADD or SUBTRACT | | |
| Non-Print, Const., Skilled | CEAN01 | 16 |
| Non-Print, Const., Unskilled | CEAN02 | 22 |
| Non-Print, Per Number - S | CEAN03 | 29 |
| Non-Print, Per Number - U | CEAN04 | 39 |
| Print, Const., Skilled | CEAP01 | 21 |
| Print, Const., Unskilled | CEAP02 | 30 |
| Print, Per Number - S | CEAP03 | 29 |
| Print, Per Number - U | CEAP04 | 39 |
| DIVIDE or MULTIPLY | | |
| Non-Print, Skilled | CEDN01 | 66 |
| Non-Print, Unskilled | CEDN02 | 91 |
| Print, Skilled | CEDP01 | 126 |
| Print, Unskilled | CEDP02 | 191 |
| MENTALLY | | |
| ADD PER NUMBER | CMAN | 108 |
| DIVIDE (Q × d) | CMDN | 131 |
| MULTIPLY (M × m) | CMMN | 66 |
| SUBTRACT the COLUMN | CMSC | 51 |

### D — DUPLICATE

| | | |
|---|---|---|
| XEROX | | |
| FIRST COPY | | |
| 2400 MODEL | DXFFM01 | 430 |
| 3600/7000 MODEL | DXFFM02 | 440 |
| ADD'L X, FASTER | | |
| 2400 MODEL | DXFAM01 | 257 |
| 3600/7000 MODEL | DXFAM02 | 267 |
| ADD'L COPIES | | |
| 2400 MODEL | DXAC01 | 42 |
| 3600/7000 MODEL | DXAC02 | 28 |

### E — EYE TIMES

| | | |
|---|---|---|
| DECIDE SIMPLE | EDS | 11 |
| DECIDE COMPLEX | EDC | 89 |
| READ PER INCH | ERI | 1 |
| READ DIGIT ALOUD | ERDA | 11 |
| READ DIGIT SILENT | ERDS | 7 |
| READ WORD ALOUD | ERWA | 11 |
| READ WORD SILENT | ERW6 | 5 |
| SCAN FORM | ESF | 11 |

### F — FASTEN/UNFASTEN

| | | |
|---|---|---|
| BINDER | | |
| ADD | | |
| FASTEN | FBAF | 103 |
| UNFASTEN | FBAU | 70 |
| DO-TANG | | |
| FASTEN | FBDF | 126 |
| UNFASTEN | FBDU | 77 |
| SPIRAL | | |
| OPEN | FBSO | 92 |
| CLOSE | FBSC | 17 |
| THREE RING | | |
| OPEN | FBTO | 31 |
| CLOSE | FBTC | 31 |
| CLIP | | |
| PAPER | | |
| PLACE | FCPP | 75 |
| REMOVE | FCPR | 43 |
| TWO-PRONG | | |
| PLACE | FCTP | 95 |
| REMOVE | FCTR | 66 |
| PIN | | |
| PLACE | FPP | 133 |
| REMOVE | FPR | 70 |
| RUBBER BAND | | |
| PLACE | FRP | 129 |
| REMOVE | FRR | 16 |
| STAPLE | | |
| HAND | | |
| FIRST | FSHF | 77 |
| ADDITIONAL | FSHA | 36 |
| TABLE | | |
| FIRST | FSTF | 37 |
| ADDITIONAL | FSTA | 20 |
| REMOVE | | |
| FIRST | FSRF | 84 |
| ADDITIONAL | FSRA | 52 |
| TAPE | | |
| CELLOPHANE | | |
| PLACE | FTCP | 109 |
| REMOVE | FTCR | 57 |

### G — GET and ASIDE

| | | |
|---|---|---|
| GET ONLY | | |
| BATCH OF PAPERS (loose) | GGB | 31 |
| JUMBLED OBJECT | GGJ | 27 |
| MEDIUM OBJECT | GGM | 18 |
| SHEET OF PAPER | GGS | 21 |
| ASIDE ONLY | | |
| TO FIXTURE | GAF | 23 |
| TO OTHER HAND | GAH | 20 |
| TO PILE | GAP | 32 |
| TO TABLE | GAT | 15 |
| COMBINED GET & ASIDE | | |
| BATCH-TO-FIXTURE | GBF | 54 |
| BATCH-TO-PILE | GBP | 63 |
| BATCH-TO-TABLE | GBT | 46 |
| JUMBLED TO FIXTURE | GJF | 50 |
| JUMBLED TO OTHER HAND | GJH | 47 |
| JUMBLED TO TABLE | GJT | 42 |
| MEDIUM TO FIXTURE | GMF | 41 |
| MEDIUM TO OTHER HAND | GMH | 38 |
| MEDIUM TO TABLE | GMT | 33 |

## G GET and ASIDE (Cont'd.)

| Element | Code | TMU |
|---|---|---|
| SHEET TO FIXTURE | GSF | 44 |
| SHEET TO OTHER HAND | GSH | 41 |
| SHEET TO PILE | GSP | 53 |
| SHEET TO TABLE | GST | 36 |

## H HANDLE PAPER

| Element | Code | TMU |
|---|---|---|
| CUT (Hand Cutter) | | |
| FIRST CUT | HCF | 66 |
| ADDITIONAL CUT | HCA | 48 |
| DRILL | | |
| HOLE | HDH | 115 |
| SET GUIDE (1) | HDS | 26 |
| FOLD (Per Fold) | | |
| GREAT CARE | | |
| NORMAL MATERIAL | HFG01 | 84 |
| HEAVY MATERIAL | HFG02 | 101 |
| NO CARE | | |
| NORMAL MATERIAL | HFN01 | 44 |
| HEAVY MATERIAL | HFN02 | 62 |
| SOME CARE | | |
| NORMAL MATERIAL | HFS01 | 63 |
| HEAVY MATERIAL | HFS02 | 79 |
| JOG | | |
| LARGE | | |
| UP TO 1" THICK | HJO01 | 5 |
| OVER 1" THICK | HJO02 | 9 |
| SHEETS | | |
| UP TO 1" THICK | HJB01 | 8 |
| OVER 1" THICK | HJB02 | 12 |
| PUNCH | | |
| SPIRAL BINDING | HPS | 47 |
| THREE HOLE | HPT | 30 |
| SHIFT | | |
| FLIP OR TURN | HSF | 23 |
| GENERAL | HSG | 27 |
| TEAR | | |
| CARE | HTC | 32 |
| NO CARE | HTN | 23 |
| UNFOLD (Per Fold) | HU | 30 |

## I INSERT

| Element | Code | TMU |
|---|---|---|
| CARD | | |
| PLACE | | |
| EASY | | |
| NO-TILT | ICPE01 | 133 |
| TILT | ICPE02 | 82 |
| AVERAGE | | |
| NO-TILT | ICPA01 | 188 |
| TILT | ICPA02 | 62 |
| DIFFICULT | | |
| NO-TILT | ICPD01 | 242 |
| TILT | ICPD02 | 132 |
| REMOVE | | |
| EASY | | |
| NO-TILT | ICRE01 | 117 |
| TILT | ICRE02 | 137 |
| AVERAGE | | |
| NO-TILT | ICRA01 | 162 |
| TILT | ICRA02 | 82 |
| DIFFICULT | | |
| NO-TILT | ICRD01 | 227 |
| TILT | ICRD02 | 209 |

## I INSERT (Cont'd.)

| Element | Code | TMU |
|---|---|---|
| FOLDER | | |
| PLACE | | |
| EASY | | |
| NO-TILT | IFPE01 | 168 |
| TILT | IFPE02 | 91 |
| AVERAGE | | |
| NO-TILT | IFPA01 | 227 |
| TILT | IFPA02 | 102 |
| DIFFICULT | | |
| NO-TILT | IFPD01 | 333 |
| TILT | IFPD02 | 198 |
| REMOVE | | |
| EASY | | |
| NO-TILT | IFRE01 | 151 |
| TILT | IFRE02 | 178 |
| AVERAGE | | |
| NO-TILT | IFRA01 | 210 |
| TILT | IFRA02 | 237 |
| DIFFICULT | | |
| NO-TILT | IFRD01 | 291 |
| TILT | IFRD02 | 344 |
| MATERIAL | | |
| BINDER | | |
| ACCO | IMBA | 65 |
| DUO-TANG | IMBD | 136 |
| SPIRAL | IMBS | 58 |
| THREE RING | IMBT | 86 |
| CUTTER | | |
| HAND | IMCH | 39 |
| DRILL or PUNCH | IMDP | 36 |

## L LOCATE

| Element | Code | TMU |
|---|---|---|
| CARD | | |
| GENERAL | LCG | 40 |
| APPROXIMATE | LCA | 22 |
| SPECIFIC | LCS | 14 |
| FOLDER | | |
| GENERAL | LFG | 48 |
| APPROXIMATE | LFA | 31 |
| SPECIFIC | LFS | 18 |
| GENERAL | | |
| FAN | LGF | 4 |
| THUMB | LGT | 10 |
| IDENTIFY | | |
| EASY | LIE | 28 |
| DIFFICULT | LID | 35 |
| PAGE | | |
| BOUND | | |
| EASY | LPBE | 134 |
| AVERAGE | LPBA | 187 |
| DIFFICULT | LPBD | 313 |
| LOOSE | | |
| EASY | LPLE | 147 |
| AVERAGE | LPLA | 221 |
| DIFFICULT | LPLD | 334 |

## K KEYSTROKES

| Element | Code | TMU |
|---|---|---|
| ALPHA | | |
| LINEAR | | |
| TWO HANDS | | |
| SKILLED | KALTS | 4.0 |
| UNSKILLED | KALTU | 5.6 |
| FUNCTIONAL | | |
| ONE HAND | | |
| SKILLED | KFLOS | 6.6 |
| UNSKILLED | KFLOU | 10.4 |
| TWO HANDS | | |
| SKILLED | KFLTS | 6.2 |
| UNSKILLED | KFLTU | 9.3 |
| TEN | | |
| ONE HAND | | |
| SKILLED | KFT0S | 5.2 |
| UNSKILLED | KFT0U | 7.9 |
| NUMERIC | | |
| LINEAR | | |
| ONE HAND | | |
| SKILLED | KNLOS | 5.2 |
| UNSKILLED | KNLOU | 7.9 |
| TEN | | |
| ONE HAND | | |
| SKILLED | KNT0S | 4.0 |
| UNSKILLED | KNT0U | 5.6 |
| SPECIAL | | |
| ONE HAND | | |
| SKILLED | KSOS | 8.4 |
| UNSKILLED | KSOU | 13.0 |

## M MAILING

| Element | Code | TMU |
|---|---|---|
| FOLD | | |
| NO SEAL | | |
| INSERT | | |
| REGULAR ENVELOPE | MFN01 | 195 |
| MANILA ENVELOPE | MFN02 | 240 |
| STRINGED ENVELOPE | MFN03 | 226 |
| SEAL | | |
| REGULAR ENVELOPE | MFS01 | 275 |
| MANILA ENVELOPE | MFS02 | 340 |
| IDENTIFY | | |
| LABEL-STICKER | | |
| DRY | MIL01 | 49 |
| WET | MIL02 | 85 |
| STAMP | | |
| SELF-STICK | MIS01 | 13 |
| SELF-LICKING | MIS02 | 56 |
| DATE SET | MIS03 | 49 |
| OPEN | | |
| SEALED | | |
| REGULAR ENVELOPE | MOSF01 | 192 |
| MANILA ENVELOPE | MOSF02 | 199 |
| UNFOLDED | | |
| REGULAR ENVELOPE | MOSU01 | 132 |
| MANILA ENVELOPE | MOSU02 | 169 |

## M MAILING (Cont'd.)

| Element | Code | TMU |
|---|---|---|
| UNFOLDED | | |
| INSERT | | |
| SEAL | | |
| REGULAR ENVELOPE | MUS01 | 130 |
| MANILA ENVELOPE | MUS02 | 258 |
| NO-SEAL | | |
| REGULAR ENVELOPE | MUN01 | 50 |
| MANILA ENVELOPE | MUN02 | 168 |
| STRINGED ENVELOPE | MUN03 | 145 |

## O OPEN AND CLOSE

| Element | Code | TMU |
|---|---|---|
| BINDER | | |
| COVER | | |
| 8½ x 11 | OBC01 | 48 |
| 11 x 17 | OBC02 | 73 |
| DRAWERS AND DOORS | | |
| DESK DRAWER | ODD | 62 |
| FILE DRAWER | ODF | 78 |
| HANDLE TYPE DOOR | ODH | 74 |
| KNOB TYPE DOOR | ODK | 53 |
| LATCH TYPE DOOR | ODL | 68 |
| SWINGING DOOR | ODS | 21 |
| FILE | | |
| FOLLOWER | OFF | 98 |
| TOPS | | |
| CAPS | OTC | 106 |
| FLAPS | OTF | 95 |
| HINGED LID | OTH | 35 |
| LID | OTL | 71 |
| STOPPER | OTS | 69 |

## P POST

| Element | Code | TMU |
|---|---|---|
| ADDRESS | | |
| COMPLETE | | |
| BUSINESS | PAC01 | 2110 |
| PERSONAL | PAC02 | 1069 |
| NAME ONLY | PAN | 399 |
| STREET ONLY | PAS | 313 |
| Town, State & Zip Only | PAT | 397 |
| DATE | | |
| ALPHA AND NUMERIC | PDA | 281 |
| NUMERIC ONLY | PDN | 144 |
| INITIALS | PI | 83 |
| LINE (12 Words) | | |
| EASY | PLE | 977 |
| DIFFICULT | PLD | 1040 |
| NUMBER | | |
| AMOUNT | PNA | 129 |
| THREE DIGITS | PNT | 71 |
| SIX DIGITS | PNS | 132 |
| NINE DIGITS | PNN | 193 |
| WORD | | |
| EASY | PWE | 90 |
| DIFFICULT | PWD | 96 |

## R READ

| Element | Code | TMU |
|---|---|---|
| ADDRESS | | |
| COMPLETE | | |
| BUSINESS | RAC01 | 119 |
| PERSONAL | RAC02 | 77 |
| NAME ONLY | RAN | 21 |
| STREET ONLY | RAS | 28 |
| TOWN, STATE & ZIP | RAT | 28 |
| DATE | | |
| ALPHABETIC | RDA | 19 |
| NUMERICAL | RDN | 14 |
| LINE | | |
| EASY | RLE | 60 |
| DIFFICULT | RLD | 132 |
| NUMBER/AMOUNT | | |
| EASY TO LOCATE | RNE | 14 |
| DIFFICULT TO LOCATE | RND | 47 |
| WORD | | |
| EASY | RWE | 5 |
| DIFFICULT | RWD | 11 |

## T TYPE

| Element | Code | TMU |
|---|---|---|
| ADDRESS | | |
| BUSINESS | | |
| SKILLED | TAB01 | 622 |
| UNSKILLED | TAB02 | 862 |
| PERSONAL | | |
| SKILLED | TAP01 | 368 |
| UNSKILLED | TAP02 | 427 |
| CITY, STATE & ZIP CODE | | |
| SKILLED | TAC01 | 114 |
| UNSKILLED | TAC02 | 196 |
| NAME ONLY | | |
| SKILLED | TAN01 | 114 |
| UNSKILLED | TAN02 | 198 |
| STREET ONLY | | |
| SKILLED | TAS01 | 94 |
| UNSKILLED | TAS02 | 129 |
| DATE | | |
| ALPHABETICALLY | | |
| SKILLED | TDA01 | 66 |
| UNSKILLED | TDA02 | 93 |
| NUMERIC | | |
| SKILLED | TDN01 | 28 |
| UNSKILLED | TDN02 | 39 |
| ERROR CORRECTION | | |
| AUTOMATIC STRIP | TEAS | 38 |
| ERASE COMPOSITE | TEEC | 352 |
| LIQUID COMPOSITE | TELC | 367 |
| STRIP COMPOSITE | TESC | 135 |
| INITIALS | | |
| SKILLED | TIS | 18 |
| UNSKILLED | TIU | 26 |
| LINE (6) | | |
| SKILLED | TLS | 308 |
| UNSKILLED | TLU | 427 |
| NUMBER | | |
| AMOUNT | | |
| SKILLED | TNA01 | 34 |
| UNSKILLED | TNA02 | 49 |
| NUMBER ONLY (6 Digits) | | |
| SKILLED | TNN01 | 24 |
| UNSKILLED | TNN02 | 34 |

## T TYPE (Cont'd.)

| Element | Code | TMU |
|---|---|---|
| OPENING AND CLOSING | | |
| BUSINESS | | |
| SKILLED | TOB01 | 1217 |
| UNSKILLED | TOB02 | 1629 |
| PERSONAL | | |
| SKILLED | TOP01 | 903 |
| UNSKILLED | TOP02 | 1191 |
| MEMO | | |
| SKILLED | TOM01 | 568 |
| UNSKILLED | TOM02 | 708 |
| PREPARE | | |
| INDENTATION SET | TPI02 | 35 |
| MARGINS SET | TPM02 | 86 |
| PLACE AND REMOVE PAPER | TPP08 | 289 |
| TABS SET | | |
| FIRST | TPT01 | 51 |
| ADDITIONAL | TPT02 | 22 |
| RETURN CARRIAGE | | |
| CLEAR | TPTS3 | 37 |
| ELECTRIC | TRE | 14 |
| INDEX | TRI | 4 |
| TABULATE | | |
| FIRST TAB | TTF | 12 |
| ADDITIONAL TABS | TTA | 5 |
| SPECIAL | | |
| Allowance for Transcription (Times Typing) | TSAT | 1.06. |
| Error (Per Error) | TSATE | 694 |

## W WRITE

| Element | Code | TMU |
|---|---|---|
| DIGIT (per Digit) | WD | 19 |
| LETTER (Print) | | |
| LOWER CASE | WLL | 19 |
| UPPER CASE | WLU | 24 |
| PUNCTUATION | WP | 15 |
| WRITE (Long Hand) | | |
| LOWER CASE | WWL | 15 |
| UPPER CASE | WWU | 22 |
| SINGLE PURPOSE DATA | | |
| COMPLETE ADDRESS | | |
| BUSINESS | WSA | 120 |
| PERSONAL | WS001 | 1941 |
| NAME ONLY | WS002 | 962 |
| STREET ONLY | WS003 | 328 |
| TOWN, STATE & ZIP ONLY | WS004 | 275 |
| DATE | | |
| ALPHABETIC | WS005 | 368 |
| NUMERIC | WS001 | 220 |
| INITIALS | WSI | 130 |
| LINE (12 Words) | | |
| NO COMPOSITION | WSL01 | 96 |
| COMPOSITION | WSL02 | 937 |
| NUMBER | | |
| THREE DIGITS | WSN01 | 1290 |
| SIX DIGITS | WSN02 | 54 |
| NINE DIGITS | WSN03 | 108 |
| WORD | | |
| NO COMPOSITION | WSW01 | 162 |
| COMPOSITION | WSW02 | 78 |

## TIME CONVERSION TABLE

1 UNIT = .00001 hour
= .0006 minute
= .036 second